Beyond Thatcherism

Social Policy, Politics and Society

EDITED BY
Phillip Brown and Richard Sparks

Open University Press
Milton Keynes · Philadelphia

Open University Press
Celtic Court
22 Ballmoor
Buckingham MK18 1XW

and
1900 Frost Road, Suite 101
Bristol, PA 19007, USA

First Published 1989. Reprinted 1990

British Library Cataloguing in Publication Data

Beyond Thatcherism: social policy, politics
  and society.
  1. Great Britain. Government. Social
  policies, 1979–1985
  I. Brown, Phillip, 1957–   II. Sparks,
  Richard
  361.6'1'0941

  ISBN 0-335-09904-1
  ISBN 0-335-09903-3 Pbk

Library of Congress Cataloguing-in-Publication Data

Beyond Thatcherism: social policy, politics, and society/edited by
  Phillip Brown and Richard Sparks.
    p. cm.
  Bibliography: p.
  Includes index.
  ISBN 0-335-09903-3 (pbk.)
  ISBN 0-335-09904-1 (cased)
  1. Great Britain—Social policy. 2. Great Britain—Politics and
government—1979- I. Brown, Phillip, 1957- . II. Sparks,
Richard, 1961-
HN390.B48 1989
361.6'1'0941—dc19

Typeset by GCS, Leighton Buzzard
Printed in Great Britain by Biddles Limited, Guildford & Kings Lynn

Contents

Acknowledgements

We would like to thank John Skelton from the Open University Press and all the contributors for cheerfully meeting tight deadlines. Liz Brown and Marion Smith also deserve a big 'thank you' for their enduring patience and encouragement.

Beyond Thatcherism

Notes on Contributors

Pamela Abbott is Senior Lecturer in Sociology and Social Policy at Plymouth Polytechnic. Her research interests are in health and the family. She has published a number of articles on the family and health and is joint author, with Roger Sapsford, of *Women and Social Class* and *Community Care for Mentally Handicapped Children*. She is currently writing, with Claire Wallace, *An Introduction to Sociology: Feminist Perspectives*.

David N. Ashton is Senior Lecturer in Sociology and Director of Research in the Labour Market Studies Group at the University of Leicester. He is author of many articles and is author of *Unemployment under Capitalism* (Wheatsheaf, 1986) and co-author, with D. Field, of *Young Workers* (Hutchinson, 1976) and, with M. Maguire and M. Spilsbury, *Restructuring the Labour Market* (Macmillan, 1989).

Mike Brake has taught at the universities of Bradford and Kent and was a professor of social work at Carleton University, Ottawa. He is currently a principal lecturer in the faculty of social science at the Polytechnic of North London. He has published books on radical social work, human sexuality, youth culture and comparative youth culture. He is currently engaged in writing a book, with Chris Hale, on conservative criminology during the political office of Margaret Thatcher.

Phillip Brown is a Lecturer in Sociology at the University of Kent at Canterbury. His publications include *Schooling Ordinary Kids* (Tavistock, 1987) and is co-editor with D. Ashton, of *Education, Unemployment and Labour*

Markets (Falmer, 1987) and with H. Lauder, *Education: In Search of a Future* (Falmer, 1988).

Chris Hale is a Lecturer in the Faculty of Social Sciences at the University of Kent at Canterbury. Trained as an econometrician he developed interests in criminology and published articles in *Criminology, Crime and Social Justice, British Journal of Criminology* and *Contemporary Crises*. He is currently involved in a research project analysing data from several local crime surveys and is writing a book with Mike Brake on the Conservative Party's law and order policy since 1979.

Christopher C. Harris is Professor of Sociology at the University College of Swansea. His main interests lie in the sociology of the family, social theory, and the sociology of economic life. His publications include *The Family and Social Change* (with Colin Rosser, 1965), *The Family* (1969), *Fundamental Concepts and the Sociological Enterprise* (1980), *The Family and Industrial Society* (1983) and *Redundancy and Recession* (1987).

Ray Jobling is a Lecturer in Sociology at the University of Cambridge and fellow of St John's College. He was formerly editor of the journal *Sociology of Health and Illness* and his research interests lie in the sociology of medicine, education and employment. He has been active for many years in health politics and is chair both of a major support organization for dermatological patients and of Cambridge Community Health Council.

Mark Kleinman is a Research Associate at the Department of Land Economy, Cambridge University and a Fellow of Wolfson College. He has written widely on housing issues and is co-author of *Private Rented Housing in the 1980s and 1990s* (Granta Editions, Cambridge, 1988).

Mark Mitchell is Principal Lecturer in Sociology and Acting Head of the School of Social and Historical Studies, Portsmouth Polytechnic. His previous publications include articles on social theory and, with Dave Russell, various articles and papers on aspects of current South African politics. Currently, his research interests include work on critical theory, the state and current politics in South Africa and Southern Africa, and researching anti-racist professional practice in Britain.

Sarah Monk is an economist specializing in urban and regional problems. She taught housing economics at several London polytechnics before joining the Department of Land Economy at Cambridge University to do research into various aspects of land use. She is joint author of a book on property and industrial development, and is currently looking at the impact of local authority investment in firms as a way of boosting the local economy.

Mike Nellis is a lecturer in Social Work (criminal justice) at Sheffield University, with a long-standing interest in juvenile crime. He has worked as a generic social worker and as an Intermediate Treatment Officer and is currently working on a thesis on the historical development of Intermediate Treatment in England and Wales.

Dave Russell is a Senior Lecturer in Sociology, School of Social and Historical Studies, Portsmouth Polytechnic. His previous publications include (with Mark Mitchell) various articles and papers on aspects of current South African politics. Current interests include work on the state and current politics in South Africa and Southern Africa and researching anti-racist professional practice in Britain. He is actively involved in developing courses in anti-racism for state professional employees, especially social workers, nurses and other ancillary workers and policy officers.

Richard Sparks is a Research Associate at the Institute of Criminology, University of Cambridge where he is engaged in ethnographic fieldwork in long-term prisons. He has written various articles on crime in the media, fear of crime and the politics of censorship. He is currently completing a thesis about violence on television.

Ian Taylor is Professor of Sociology at the University of Salford and was formerly Professor of Sociology at Carleton University, Ottawa. He is author/editor of six books on criminological theory, plus some fifty published articles. His recent work has included a critical analysis of Canadian current affairs television and video violence.

Claire Wallace is Senior Lecturer in Sociology and Social Policy, Plymouth Polytechnic. She has been writing and researching in the area of youth, employment and unemployment for some years, and also in the area of work and the household with Ray Pahl. Her book is entitled *For Richer For Poorer: Growing up In and Out of Work* (Routledge, 1987). She is currently writing a book about youth in society and also a feminist introduction to sociology, with Pamela Abbott.

Editors' Introduction

In the wake of Mrs Thatcher's third election victory, one might ask whether there is anything 'beyond' Thatcherism. She is already the longest serving Prime Minister this century, and shows few signs of abandoning her political and moral crusade, which includes the removal of socialism from the British political landscape. Moreover, although the ideas which inform Thatcherism date back to the last century, her beliefs and policies appear both novel and innovative when set against the political consensus and social democratic policies of the 1960s.

Thatcherism has challenged much of the received wisdom of the post-war consensus. It has achieved popular appeal by identifying collectivist economic and social policies as being mainly responsible for Britain's industrial decline and social decay. However, opponents of Thatcherism have so far been unable to mount a credible alternative, not simply because of the political cunning of the Tories, but because the social and economic policies at the centre of post-war reconstruction were already in crisis by the mid-1970s as world recession and unemployment gripped Britain.

The Welfare State has not fulfilled the more optimistic expectations which were held out for it, such as the abolition of poverty, unemployment and educational inequalities. It is for this reason that thinking beyond Thatcherism has proved to be that much more difficult, because its defeat cannot be secured by simply calling for a return to earlier models. To go beyond Thatcherism we will require new policy alternatives, and it is towards this goal that this volume is dedicated.

Thatcherism and the New Right

> Thatcherism is essentially an instinct, a series of moral values and an approach to leadership rather than an ideology.... The same themes have cropped up again and again in speeches and interviews throughout the past decade – personal responsibility, the family and national pride. The key lies in her use of language ... words like freedom, self-respect, independence, initiative, choice, conviction, duty, greatness, heart and faith recur (Riddell, 1985: 7).

The language of freedom, personal responsibility and choice is set against a vision of the decadent 1960s and the socialist 'block mentality', 'tower blocks, trade union block votes, block schools' (Thatcher, 1988). It is asserted that the socialist ideals which underpinned post-war reconstruction had also led to a culture of dependence rather than a culture of enterprise, and that in consequence Britain was in social, economic and moral decline. Thatcherism is therefore dedicated to destroying socialism:

> For my first 25 years in politics it was socialist ideas that were influencing Conservatives. But the world has seen Socialism now, and it is not for free human beings, it is not for the British character. It produces neither prosperity nor human dignity. As you know, it is not the opposition I want to get rid of, it is central planning and control, the centrally-controlled, Socialist society in which your rights come from the government and you do as you are told (Thatcher, 1987).

Mrs Thatcher has recently begun to style Britain as the 'first post-socialist society'. As an historical claim this is mumbo-jumbo, crass and confused. As a self-confident, polemical assertion, however, it has a certain potency. Mrs Thatcher's aim here is to offer a revisionist history of British society which rejects the equation of socialism with social progress, by defining socialism as an intrusion, or deviation from the path of things inherently British. Collectivism was a discrete episode, even perhaps a necessary one under the exigencies of post-war reconstruction, but it is now obsolete.

Any account of Thatcherism must include a consideration of the 'Thatcher factor', which recognizes her strong personality and a leadership style which is both self-confident and dogmatic. She has little time or regard for those who disagree with her, and as one of her supporters has noted, she has 'a certain impatience with subtlety of feeling, a lack of sympathy with people unlike her and a definitely limited range of experience' (Riddell, 1985: 9). Nevertheless, despite her leadership style and lack of experience about what life is like for the more disadvantaged sections of the British population, she has been very successful in communicating the populist themes of Thatcherism to the electorate (see Hall and Jacques, 1983). Thatcherism continues to gain political advantage from what to an observer may look like inconsistencies: they provide for a tactical flexibility which allows Thatcherism's proponents to move between arguments about economic freedom and social discipline without visible difficulty. This is a significant feature of what Harris (Chapter 1, this volume) calls Thatcherite 'statecraft'. The keywords of Thatcherism (freedom, choice, self-reliance and enterprise on the one hand; morality, responsibility and nationhood on the other) are both resonant and vague. They are likely to be differentially received and accorded different weight and priority across the range of individuals and social groups to whom they are addressed. There is an enormous social distance between the economic libertarianism and spectacular consumption of some young professionals on the one hand, and the moral anxiety of a Mary Whitehouse on the other – yet the Thatcherite package is capable of incorporating them both. Or so it appears for the time being.

It is part of the argument of this book that the amoeba-like reach of the Thatcherite project, which has made many critics and opponents despair of overcoming it, in fact makes it more vulnerable than it appears. Not all of those who have supported, or acquiesced in, the development of Thatcherism over the last decade have done so for the same reasons or with equal commitment. We are not 'all Thatcherite now'. A significant number of people who voted Conservative in the last three general elections, did so primarily because of the absence of a credible alternative party, not because of a whole-hearted commitment to the politics of Thatcherism.

The contention, evident in the above quotation from Riddell, that along with her leadership style, Thatcherism is essentially an instinct and a series of moral values, should not obscure the fact that Thatcherism is founded on ideology. It is rooted in a combination of 'neo-liberalism' and 'authoritarian conservatism', which are deployed in albeit contradictory ways. This fact is of major importance because, as Riddell correctly points out, 'when it comes to policy Mrs Thatcher has not been an original thinker. Most of the Conservative Party's programme has come initially from other people: her contribution has been to take up and articulate these themes' (Riddell, 1985:8–9).

These 'other people' have been New Right intellectuals associated with a number of right-wing pressure groups and 'think-tanks' such as the Centre for Policy Studies (which was established by Sir Keith Joseph and Mrs Thatcher), and the Institute of Economic Affairs. Thatcherism, therefore, represents an important ideological shift within the Conservative Party, although it cannot be equated with the New Right because 'even in Britain the New Right is broader and more varied than a particular set of policies or style of government' (Levitas, 1986:1). In this volume, the term New Right (see Levitas, 1986; Hall and Jacques, 1983) will refer both to ideas and policies which stem from 'neo-liberalism', which Gamble (1983) has characterized in terms of 'markets good, government bad', and from a form of 'authoritarian conservatism' with its emphasis upon hierarchy, authority and nation:

> The New Right is the seedbed from which Thatcherism has grown and is composed of two rather different strands. There is the revival of liberal political economy, which seeks the abandonment of Keynesianism and any kinds of government intervention; and there is a new populism – the focusing on issues like immigration, crime and punishment, strikes, social security abuse, taxation and bureaucracy.... The real innovation of Thatcherism is the way it has linked traditional Conservative concerns with the basis of authority in social institutions and the importance of internal order and external security, with a new emphasis upon re-establishing free markets and extending market criteria into new fields (Levitas, 1986:6).

Throughout this volume, it will become evident that the ideologies of the New Right inform Thatcherism in many areas of contemporary social and economic policy, but they do so in often contradictory and inconsistent ways, and this offers a clear opportunity to begin to argue against them. To contest this rhetoric is to argue not only that the things which Thatcherism holds up as values are questionable, but also that they operate in contradiction, they cannot all be realized together and are often mutually exclusive: you cannot have one *and* the other.

The recognition of areas of possible contradiction, such that different areas of the Thatcherite agenda work in antagonism with one another, offers opportunities for new and well focussed alternative thinking. The fact is that the object to be analysed, Thatcherism, is complex and uneven, rather than a unitary bloc of consistent beliefs. The resulting contradictions and inconsistencies in the 'seedbed' of Thatcherism provide an opportunity to undermine Thatcherism (in its own terms). For example, the relationship which Thatcherism envisages between the individual and the State is misconceived. Thatcherism's commitment to individualism, expressed mainly at the level of choice in consumption, means that its implicit social theory is little more than an elaboration of classical economics (cf. Marquand, 1988). Thatcherism is thus avowedly anti-collectivist, yet a number of its key terms, such as nation and community, necessarily presuppose collectivities. This results in a disregard of – even hostility to – the institutions which mediate between individuals and these larger collectivities. The attempt to reference notions of nationhood and community aims to reinstate, in ideology, arenas which Thatcherite practice undermines. Those intermediate agencies which are still recognized, principally the family and to some extent education, are called upon to bear a weight quite out of proportion to their empirical basis. It is an inherent feature of Thatcherism to protest against social trends which are of its own making and to castigate social institutions for failing to live up to the Thatcherite vision. This inattention to what Dahrendorf (1985:121) calls 'institution building' (by which he means the development of social arrangements which mediate between individual and society), leads to a contradiction in Thatcherism's moral language, because 'if there is no such thing as society' (as Mrs Thatcher has suggested), what is to be the basis of social order? This problem is examined in detail by Harris in Chapter 1. Moreover, whereas some areas of social policy and service provision are subsumed under market imperatives (for example, the privatization of transport, utilities and education) others, such as the regulation of sexuality and the family, are directed by moral declaration.

Harris (Chapter 1) will also make clear that the neo-liberal, 'minimal' state is no less coercive than its predecessors. Indeed, in some areas it is markedly more so. The conjunction of economic deregulation with public commitment to law and order, the family and social propriety concentrates state activities in areas of policing and surveillance. Thus, to take two examples, in the City and in the deregulated media (especially videos and now satellite broadcasting), the Government steps in to curb and censure a disorganization which results from the very process of unleashing market forces.

It is important for those who are concerned, even dismayed, by these developments to elaborate perspectives in which the languages of fact, reason and commitment are more closely and intelligibly integrated. The essays collected in this book seek to do this. The much-vaunted third-term 'radicalism' of the latest Thatcher administration is marked by its increased attention to social policy initiatives. The opening up of social policy to market interventions is sustained and assisted by consultations from New Right 'think-tanks'. However questionable its moral or political underpinnings, the Thatcherite appeal to managerial effectiveness in these areas is greatly bolstered by the quality of information it receives from such expert systems. The development of alternative policies, therefore, must be both similarly shrewd and plausible, as well as being more convincing at the level of moral and political justification.

With these considerations in mind, each chapter in this book focusses on a particular issue or area of policy. All of the chapters (apart from Harris, Chapter 1) broadly share a common format, i.e. they examine the impact of New Right ideology, considering both sources of popular appeal and plausibility as well as the defects which enjoin opposition to it. They also consider the consequences of New Right policies. The final section of each chapter then begins to stipulate alternative policies 'beyond Thatcherism', tenable for conditions which are likely to exist in the 1990s.

Each chapter covers areas which are, in varying degrees, in the process of transition or review. Each of them represents a contribution to debates which are already raging. The Thatcher phenomenon has already stimulated a number of extensive commentaries.[1]* The coverage we can provide is necessarily partial (essays on industrial relations, the environment, defence, and other areas clamour for inclusion). Daunting as it may be, however, the fluidity of the present situation also offers exciting space for new interventions. Those whose professional commitments are academic must now add their voice and their careful efforts to those of journalists, politicians, students, lawyers, and other citizens, prepared to think seriously about the prospects for a post-Thatcher reconstruction which will be both novel and yet able to recover all that has remained valid in the social democratic tradition. This positive intention requires a more serious effort of the sociological imagination than has been general hitherto. Thatcherism has been the most vigorous political phenomenon in Britain for the last two decades, and so merely to regret it or to disparage it in terms of models received from the past will not do. To move beyond Thatcherism is to know its dimensions well and to understand the potency of its rhetoric and actions as fully as its contradictions, weaknesses and negative social effects.

Notes

1 We refer in particular to those by Hall and Jacques (1983) and Levitas (1986). The present volume differs from these mainly in that its first priority is to relate aspects of the political 'theory' of Thatcherism to its concrete realization in specific features of social policy.

References

Dahrendorf, R. (1985). *Law and Order: The Hamlyn Lectures*. London: Stevens and Sons.

Gamble, A. (1983). Thatcherism and Conservative politics. In *The Politics of Thatcherism* (S. Hall and M. Jacques, eds). London: Lawrence and Wishart.

Hall, S. and Jacques, M. (eds) (1983). *The Politics of Thatcherism*. London: Lawrence and Wishart.

Levitas, R. (ed.) (1986). *The Ideology of the New Right*. Cambridge: Polity Press.

*Superscript numerals refer to numbered notes at the end of each chapter.

Marquand, D. (1988). Richesse oblige: The new Tory wave. *New Statesman*, 3 June, pp. 21-2.

Riddell, P. (1985). *The Thatcher Government*. Oxford: Blackwell.

Thatcher, M. (1987). *The Independent*, 14 September.

Thatcher, M. (1988). *The Daily Mail*, 29 April.

1   The State and the Market

Christopher C. Harris

Mrs Thatcher is a practising politician, not a political philosopher or theorist. Thatcherism has therefore to be constructed from the amalgam of views, prejudices, values, concepts, policies and decisions with which she is associated. It is too much to expect that all these elements will form a consistent pattern. This chapter does not proceed therefore by examining them, but concentrates on a pair of allegedly opposed concepts without which the whole of the Thatcherite political experiment would fail to make any sense. The choice of this pair of concepts – the State and the market – enables us to locate the Thatcherite enterprise in terms of contemporary trends in political thought, for she has been heavily influenced by the ideas of a group of thinkers both here and in the United States who are currently termed the 'New Right'.

The New Right have succeeded in redefining the central political issue. For them, the issue is *not* what should the State be used for, but the extent to which social and economic life should be regulated and controlled by the State. To answer this question, the New Right has resurrected the late eighteenth- and early nineteenth-century arguments of the classical political economists against State intervention and control. These arguments were of course concerned with the inappropriateness of the sort of governmental control exercised over the economy in the late seventeenth and early eighteenth centuries to the conditions of the developing and industrializing economy of the early nineteenth century. Before the New Right, these arguments were regarded as being totally inappropriate to a technologically advanced capitalist economy in the late twentieth century. The classical doctrine held that the State was an anachronistic institution and that its regulative functions would be replaced in the new industrial society of the future by the market. The

New Right does not take the view that this doctrine is only valid in the historical context in which it originated, but holds, rather, that it is an absolute truth and that the social and economic problems of post-war Britain derive from the refusal of both major political parties to recognize this fact.

The classical doctrine which originates from Adam Smith (1776), argues for a minimal state concerned only with defence, law and the provision of public utilities (e.g. roads). To this list is usually added the maintenance of a stable currency and the control of such private actions as may have public effects (externalities), e.g. environmental pollution. Even if the reduction of State activity to these spheres is possible in contemporary society, it was not a viable option for any government in 1979. Thatcherism, therefore, differs from the New Right in that it is not a political theory but a set of policies, attitudes and tendencies developed under very specific historical conditions, which are informed by the central meaning of New Right philosophy – State control and intervention is evil and the unregulated operation of markets is good.

The question which must now be addressed is why a rising Tory politician in the 1970s should have taken over a set of ideas which appeared to most people to be extreme, anachronistic and irrelevant and should have succeeded in using them to shift the whole political ground and make this new terrain the site of successive electoral successes.

Thatcherism as statecraft

Rather than attempt to return to the 1770s, Mrs Thatcher's espousal of the State-market opposition seems to be an attempt to repeat at a more profound level the policies of the first post-war Conservative administration which, in reaction to 10 years of austerity, rationing and controls, had campaigned under the slogan 'set the people free'. The market side of the opposition, for electoral purposes, was given a populist rather than an economic meaning. Thatcherism is a form of populism which mirrors, on the right, the Bennite populism of the Labour left. The image is of a people oppressed by a coercive and restrictive State.

Mrs Thatcher's reversal of the prevailing wisdom concerning the proper balance between political and market processes, however, is not merely a matter of ideological conviction. Nor are the conversion of Sir Keith Joseph and Mrs Thatcher to the New Right, their election, their victory over their opponents in the Conservative Party, and the two subsequent election successes of the Conservatives merely matters of political chance and personal charisma. They are the result of a realistic judgement concerning the prerequisites of gaining and retaining power under the economic and social conditions of the late 1970s and 1980s. They are not the result of ideology but of a theory of *statecraft*.

In an extremely perceptive article, Jim Bulpitt has argued that prior to Thatcherism the Conservative Party had pursued a statecraft which involved a commitment to winning power at the centre, the willingness to take on as clients any interest group which seemed likely to assist them in achieving that aim and, once in office, the attempt to achieve autonomy for the centre 'on those matters which they defined as "high politics" at any particular time' (Bulpitt, 1986:27). The philosophy behind this statecraft was that government was the job of an insulated élite. During the 1960s this stance became increasingly difficult to maintain in the face of an increasing need to manage the economy and hence to control powerful groups within society. Specifically, the successful pursuit of macro-economic policies (demand regulation and the management of the balance of payments) required the control of wages and incomes. The Heath administration failed dismally in this regard and allowed Wilson's Labour Party to claim that it alone had a domestic policy which could deliver that which was required.

The Thatcher revolution consisted in refusing to play the domestic policy game. Whereas other politicians were continuing to struggle with the problem of domestic economic policy in the fight to control inflation, Mrs Thatcher and Sir Keith Joseph latched on to 'monetarism' – the belief that prices could be controlled by controlling the money supply – and they did so as a way of returning to the traditional Conservative *statecraft* of domestic non-intervention. If the first duty of the State could be presented as ensuring the soundness of money and all other economic decisions as flowing from that objective, then the way is open for taking contentious decisions out of politics and thus giving politicians a certain autonomy from other groups within society. Intervention was to be replaced by 'arm's length government', which accorded reciprocal autonomy to the institutions with which the Government had no wish to interfere. Unfortunately, the reciprocal autonomy strategy was to allow 'important groups and institutions to pursue policies inimical to the successful achievement of its macro economic strategy and, therefore, the centre's own relative autonomy' (Bulpitt, 1986:38) and, as a result, after 1980, the Government increasingly adopted a more interventionist/ control strategy towards other groups and institutions.

Bulpitt's argument that the sense in which something called Thatcherism exists, is to be found not in a coherent set of policies, 'nor in its ideas or ideology but in the realm of party statecraft' (Bulpitt, 1986: 39), may be put in the following way. The prime objective of any party is to gain and retain power. To regain power the Tory Party was required to show that it could manage the domestic economy. Since it had no strategy for such management, electoral success required that this no longer be regarded as the prime task of government. Retaining power involved avoiding a 'national rejection' of the type experienced by Heath in 1974 and Callaghan in 1979. An interventionist domestic policy results in government being blamed for all those features of social and economic life which the electorate evaluates negatively. The greater government intervention, the greater the number of dissatisfactions which can be blamed on the government and the greater the national constituency against the administration in power. Therefore, gaining and retaining power required a redefinition of the tasks of government so that they were once again capable of attainment. The achievement of the Thatcherite wing of the Conservative Party has been to carry through that redefinition. Politics in the 1970s was rapidly becoming the art of the impossible: Thatcher has succeeded in making it once again the art of the possible.

'State' and 'market' when viewed in this context acquire a new range of meanings. Rolling back the frontiers of the State involves a restriction of governmental activity to its proper sphere. The centre should attempt only to control those things which *can* be controlled from the centre – not wages and prices (directly), but taxation and government spending – thus restricting government activity to those areas in which it has some chance of success. The weakness of this strategy is the identification of that which is not the State ('civil society') with the market. The opposition between State and market is based on the opposition between the public and the private, the collective and the individual. Unfortunately for this view there are institutionalized collectivities other than the State which mediate the relation between the individual and the polity. Civil society is not composed exclusively of economically rational individuals freely pursuing their interest and profit whose freedom so to do it is the duty of government to preserve. If Britain was held to be ungovernable in the 1970s, this surely was not due *merely* to the fact that government was trying to do too much.

The institutions of the middle ground

Thatcherism tends to regard all institutions as being opposed to markets. The professions, the universities and the civil service, the trades unions, local government, the nationalized industries, the National Health Service and those institutions concerned with income maintenance, are all 'conspiracies in restraint of trade', if 'trade' be understood as the free play of market forces. These institutions continue to exist and operate even when it has been established that they are no concern of government. The way they operate cannot but be seen as a form of control: a restriction on 'choice' and the outcome of their operation cannot be assumed to facilitate as opposed to frustrate the attainment of those few objectives for which a minimalist State does take the responsibility and is electorally accountable.

Since these institutions are more powerful than individuals, it is clearly the duty of a minimalist State to minimize their interference with market forces and this requires that this new State be stronger than they are. In other words, the world must be remodelled so that civil society is identified with the market in the sense of an aggregation of freely competing individuals, even though that initially means a massive exercise in State power and eventually the emergence of the State as the only collectivity in a society of individuals. The attraction of the 'State/market' dichotomy is that it distracts attention from the sober fact that the only way for the State to abandon its traditional role of broker between the conflicting interests which constitute civil society, is to deny those interests any means of organization and articulation. That is to say, it involves the creation of what has been termed a 'mass' society (Giner, 1976). A totally free economy necessarily implies a strong State, since, if the State is the only collectivity, there will exist no source of countervailing political power. A weak State is only possible if there are no countervailing sources of power but, if they do not exist, then, by the same token, the State will be strong.

This theoretical difficulty pales into insignificance however when compared with the practical difficulties of moving in that direction at the present historical conjuncture. If we had no National Health Service, the Government would not attract to itself the odium of not funding it 'properly'. But we have such a service and even Mrs Thatcher has not so far chosen to suggest its replacement by the free market. Nor has anyone suggested that the services provided by local government should be similarly replaced or the whole apparatus of income maintenance abandoned, or that professional associations or trade unions be prohibited. Nationalized industries have been privatized but not the civil service or the universities. Moreover, part of the attraction of monetarism is that it provides a management of the economy by controlling the only economic variable that the State can (in theory) control: the public spending component of demand. However, were the economic function of the State to be restricted to defence spending and central banking, then public spending would no longer be a major influence on the economy. Were the economic frontiers of the State really to be rolled back and the institutions of public spending abolished, the chief instrument of macro-economic policies would be removed at the same time as the impediments to a truly free market.

Even electoral success and economic good fortune could not enable the Government to avoid domestic economic policy issues for ever. These forced the Government to attempt to control the institutions occupying the middle ground between the State and the market with which they had refused to bargain. Such institutions fall into three broad groups. First, there are those institutions which are part of the State apparatus: the Welfare State and the civil service. Secondly, there are those institutions which directly or indirectly are the clients of the government: local authority services, particularly education, the universities and the Health Service. Thirdly, there are institutions which are not government clients: chiefly trade unions and professional associations, but one might also add the churches.

Excluded from this list are the whole range of institutions whose function is primarily that of bargaining between interest groups or between interests and government. The Thatcher administration has seen the dismantling of these hybrids (quangos and quagos) and this must be seen as a parallel to the administration's distaste for Royal Commissions. Commissions are out of favour for three quite separate reasons: the Government does not want advice from anybody who is not 'one of us', in Mrs Thatcher's chilling phrase; she does not want information (policies are not pragmatic but principled); and, by the same token, she does not want her policies to be based on consensus (they are, rather, concerned with challenges to consensus). Royal Commissions and government-sponsored advisory bodies have, however, other functions than merely being arenas for interest bargaining and consensus production. They have an information function. Loss of this function does not matter to a truly minimalist government who would ideally only require military and macro-economic data to inform its policies. Once a government is forced to deal with the middle ground, however, it needs an information base to estimate the effects of different policy options. The poll tax is a case in point. It is not enough to frame a measure which embodies certain principles which are *a priori* desirable, given a practical or value position. It is necessary to evaluate the likely consequences of different schemes embodying those principles. This central government is not capable of doing by itself and needs to consult those whose job it will be to administer such schemes. Of course, this the Government refuses to do and, indeed, interprets reasoned argument against the detail of its measures as evidence in favour of them. As Nicholas Ridley remarked *à propos* of the poll tax (radio interview, November 1987): 'The more local authorities complain, the more convinced I am that we are right.'

The most important of the institutions of the middle ground are those occupying what we have termed the second category, i.e. 'government clients'. The Thatcherite technique for dealing with this category has been to replace bodies whose function it is to make representation or give advice to the government with bodies whose duty it is to carry out the will of the government. The National Health Service is a good illustration of the strategy. The *Guardian* identified this view clearly:

> When...Tony Newton [Moore's deputy] goes on radio or television to attack 'inefficiency' [in the health service], who is there to reply on behalf of the beleaguered service?
>
> Not apparently the chairman of the NHS management board which runs the show – because that is Mr Newton wearing another hat.
>
> Not apparently the deputy chairman of the NHS management board because he too wears another hat as the Prime Minister's personal adviser on the NHS and spear carrier for her criticisms (*Guardian*, 12 December 1987).

A former board chairman, the *Guardian* goes on to note;

favoured a more autonomous 'NHS corporation' which ministers were not prepared to tolerate because of the political sensitivity of the NHS; but nor have they accepted the consequences of being fully responsible for the organisation.

The last quotation highlights the paradoxical nature of the Thatcherite solution to the problem posed by the institutions of the middle ground. To incorporate institutions into the State prevents their becoming a rival source of power which can stand up to government. But the corollary is that if activities are controlled by the government then the government must accept responsibility for them, and it is precisely that situation that Thatcherite statecraft has sought to avoid.

The State–market opposition is inadequate because of the existence of institutions which are not part of the State but whose operation affects either the government's popularity or the success of its economic policy. It is intolerable to have one's political popularity affected by bodies one cannot control, and the proper course of action is to abolish them. However, in a modern complex society, public provision of utilities is necessarily much greater than in the eighteenth century when many of the free market ideas currently in vogue among the New Right originated, and the sphere of public provision, while it can be diminished by privatization, cannot be eliminated. Non-State public bodies were established to prevent an increase in centralized State power. Incorporating them into the State increases control, but also enlarges rather than diminishes the role of the State; it also enlarges the sphere of governmental responsibility.

The Education Bill is an example of this tendency. Dissatisfaction with education in the past can be conveniently laid at the door of local education authorities and the teaching profession (see Brown, Chapter 3, this volume). Any government is required to respond to such dissatisfaction and the decision to institute a national curriculum is one perfectly proper response. Previous governments, having made that decision, would have set up a National Curriculum Council representing groups with a legitimate interest in the curriculum. But not a Thatcher Government. There must be no statutory organization whose activities touch on those of the State which the State does not control, nor any which recognizes the legitimacy of interests other than those of the State and the (children's) parents. So the bill *itself* prescribes a national curriculum. In so doing, however, it paves the way for the electorate to lay its grievances against the new system of education at the door of the Government in the future. Having defeated the teachers and cowed the local authorities and rejected the establishment of a statutory scapegoat, the Government, thereby defined as strong, will be liable, for that very reason, to accept the full responsibility for the outcome.

What has been indicated in the foregoing discussion is an attempt by the Government, where possible, to evacuate in part some of the middle ground between State and market. However, at the same time, the Government has sought to introduce market principles within essentially bureaucratic organizations. Here the concept has been that of contract. The introduction of contracts has been mooted in respect of the civil service, but the financing of universities and the contracting out of services previously provided by direct labour has been required in the health service and is being extended to local government. Even Thatcherite administrations recognize the existence of natural monopolies in which the concept of consumer choice is not relevant. Contracting out is a way of creating market pressures to ensure the efficient provision of services by such monopolies. The State is, of course, the natural monopoly *par excellence*, and it too can be made more efficient in many of its operations by exposing it to the stimulus of market forces through the technique of contracting (Ascher, 1987).

The market as efficiency

Whereas some of the measures of the Thatcher administrations have sought to clear the middle ground by incorporation into the State or the depoliticization of issues by allowing them to be determined by the aggregation of individual choices rather than by government policy, yet others seek to restore the influence of the market to institutions which cannot then be thus dealt with. This sense of 'market' differs from the sense of freedom and choice discerned above. Indeed, its meaning is the reverse: the market as a restraint. It is scarcely possible to complain that the domestic economic policies of previous regimes were repressive. On the contrary, the existence of employee rights in terms of job protection and union membership, and free collective bargaining – barely moderated by the rhetoric of incomes policy – provided considerable freedom. These policies are seen, however, as resulting in wage inflation which needs *curbing* by increasing competition between workers, both for employment opportunities and the chance to remain in employment. The labour market needs to be '*made* to work better' by removing the institutional rigidities of employment protection, pay regulation by Wage Councils, union immunities, union strike power and the closed shop. Measures affecting all these issues were, accordingly, introduced in the Employment Acts of 1980, 1982 and 1984.

It may be doubted, however, whether these measures have had the effect that the Government intended (McInnes, 1987). Management and workers have to cooperate with one another to survive. They do not face one another as individuals in a market but as members of corporate groups whose structures have been evolved and designed to facilitate cooperation in *production*, not merely bargaining at the point of *contract*. Labour relations law, like other forms of law, is the formal means of redress of particular grievances and provides the formal framework within which substantive social relations of production develop. It is in no way to minimize the importance of law to assert that formal legal structures cannot determine the substantive content of social relations.

The need to organize production means that the demand side of the labour market is composed not of individuals – entrepreneurs and employers – but of organizations. Thatcherism seeks to bring about a shift in the economic power away from the economic institutions concerned with production in favour of the market. Exchange must determine production, not production exchange. This shift is not a movement from coercive 'government' to (free) individual choice; rather it is an attempt at coercion, to *make* the economic institutions of production change. This has as its corollary an increase in the power of employers over labour, lest their attempts to respond to market pressures are blocked by worker resistance.

Thatcherite economic policy, which involves the principle of State non-intervention and the liberation of market forces, founders because, between the State on the one hand, and the market conceived as a set of free individuals on the other, exist not only political but productive institutions without which there would be no goods to be supplied.

In social theoretical terms the conceptual space between the polity and the economy, which four generations of social thinkers have opened up in an attempt to ground a coherent conception of social life, is abolished by Thatcherism. In this sense, quite independently of any value or practical judgement concerning the social desirability of Thatcherite policy, Thatcherism and sociology are at the most basic conceptual level profoundly opposed. As Mrs Thatcher said in an interview with *Woman's Own* in 1987: 'There is no such thing as "society".'

Markets, Capital and the State

This paper has thus far attempted to work within the State–market dichotomy on which Thatcherite thought, it has been claimed, is based. Freeing ourselves of the simplicities and obscurities of the State–market dichotomy is a necessary prerequisite of post-Thatcherite reconstruction. The first step in this task is to recognize that social life is only possible as the result of institutionalized modes of cooperation, and the second is to recognize that whether social institutions hinder or facilitate the achievement of goals or objectives which are thought to be desirable will depend on the exact historical circumstances prevailing. In other words, there is nothing intrinsically inefficient or immoral about the regulation of social life by political or social institutions, nor is it necessarily better to let the market make 'decisions' about social issues than to arrive at those decisions by what has loosely been termed political processes. The 'consensus' of the post-war years regarded both extremes as highly undesirable if not impossible; we are not required to choose between a command economy on the one hand, such as that found in the Soviet Union, which allows consumers no choice of consumption pattern and hence no voice in what is produced and, on the other, an economy in which levels and patterns of consumption and production are left entirely to the operation of market forces, i.e. the unintended aggregate outcome of individual actions. The question to be faced in the future, as in the past, concerns the best balance between institutional regulation and individual choice. The answers are not determined by fundamentalist political principles of left or right, but by a detailed examination of the costs and benefits of different solutions in specific circumstances.

However, to state the matter thus fails to move far enough away from the inadequacy of the State–market opposition. The opposition implies that the reduction of State activity necessarily results in greater market choice. If this were so, privatization would produce greater consumer choice. It produces nothing of the sort. There is no reason to suppose that after denationalization, Britoil, the British Steel Corporation, British Telecom and the water authorities will provide a better service at a lower price or greater consumer choice than when publicly owned, since they will not be constrained by domestic competition. Capital expenditure will, however, no longer be financed by central government funds. This makes good electoral political sense. Government will not have to make agonizing political decisions about what fraction of the national revenues they are to receive and hence will not be liable to charges of underfunding. But privatization, while decreasing the role of the State, does nothing to impose the discipline of the market. What it does do is to subject privatized institutions to the discipline of the market for capital.

This draws attention to a further deficiency of the opposition: the unrealistic concept of what markets are. Much Thatcherite rhetoric, though lauding capitalism, seems to ignore the way in which capitalist markets work. Put very simply, it supposes that because market outcomes are the result of free individual choice, they are necessarily closer to what people want than outcomes determined by institutional processes. This proposition would only hold true if we lived in a simple world of commodity production, i.e. a world in which the object of economic activity was the production of goods; a living could not be made from the production of goods unless revenues exceeded costs; people expressed their wants by purchasing goods; and prices were proportionate to the value attached to them by consumers.

Whether or not this was ever true of the distributive, let alone the productive, branches of economic activity, it is not the case that the contemporary economy functions in this way. Any economic activity which depends even indirectly on the market for capital, is determined not only by the market in the sense of the consumer demand for the goods produced/distributed, but also by the supply of capital for that activity which is in turn determined by the relative return on the capital when so applied. Even if we ignore the artificial creation of wants by capital, it still follows that what is produced in an economy based on a market *for capital*, is not *necessarily* what 'people' (the consumer market)

[handwritten margin note: why market doesn't necessarily lead to more choice]

want, but what it is most profitable for *capital* to supply. Capital will flee from productive activities however profitable (and they cannot *be* profitable unless people want the goods produced) if there are other activities which are even more profitable. What gets produced is what makes the most profit, and this is not necessarily the same as what people most need or want.

In Thatcherite rhetoric, profit is a sign that the profit maker is making/supplying the goods that people want. The claim that 'profit' is a criterion of the social value of an economic activity fails to distinguish between two quite different propositions which can be expressed by it. One is the homely point that you cannot make a profit unless people are willing to pay for what you produce at a price which more than covers its cost. The other is the quite different claim that the social value of an economic activity is proportionate to its rate of profit. The function of the confusion between the two propositions is to legitimize the optimization of profit on the spurious grounds that the size of the profit reflects the satisfaction of the desires of consumers in the market (e.g. the controversy over British Telecom's profits and the complaints about its services). The purpose or manifest function of this confusion is to remove from government its traditional task of making judgements about the public or general good and to absolve it from all responsibility for its attainment. Its effect, or latent (ideological) function, is to legitimize the unrestrained pursuit of optimum profit.

An economy based on a free market for capital produces only those goods demanded by consumers which are maximally profitable, thus leaving other wants unfulfilled – even when their supply is profitable. In this situation the 'people' do not have a 'free choice' at all, only a choice between what the system 'decides' to produce. The differences between a free and a command economy are therefore less great than Thatcherite rhetoric would have us believe. The function of the State in a free economy should be to provide capital for productive activities which supply what the State considers to be needs which would otherwise be unmet. The effect of such State intervention would be to *increase* people's freedom of choice, not diminish it.

Such intervention would be necessary even if it was possible to supply all social needs at a profit: the State would have to capitalize *less* profitable provision. However, there is no reason whatever to suppose that demand in the economic sense reflects wants accurately. That is, there is no reason to suppose that those with genuine needs will have the income available to translate those needs into effective demand for the goods that would satisfy them. Housing is a case in point. The public provision of housing grew up as a result of the imposition of housing standards, when it was discovered that a substantial proportion of the population could not afford to pay the market price for housing which conformed to those standards. Similar considerations apply to the provision of health and education.

[handwritten margin note: people can't always afford true cost]

It does not follow, however, that the lack of market provision for specific wants or for wants of those with relatively low incomes, necessarily requires that they be supplied by the State, at either the national or local level. The opposition between *laissez-faire* and interventionism is not the same as the opposition between market and State. And here there is a lesson to be learnt from Thatcherism: responsibility to ensure provision is quite distinct from the responsibility to make provision. An active and interventionist State does not have, necessarily, to be a State which in Thatcherite terms 'does too much'. Housing does not necessarily have to be built and administered by public bodies to remedy deficiencies in the supply resulting upon the operation of market forces. One may go even further and argue that movement towards a far greater degree of intervention by the State in the operation of the free market than has previously been seen could be combined with a reduction of State provision, ownership and control.

The most obvious example of State intervention without ownership, provision or control is the institution of the marketing board. Marketing boards offer producers a stable demand at a known future price and can be combined with subsidies to encourage the production of commodities which people need but which producers find it uneconomic to produce. Intervention in market operations of this kind could well proceed hand in hand with decreased public provision. Indeed, such intervention is one way of preventing the decrease of public provision having adverse effects on those sections of society which exercise the least market power.

It is one of the ironies and paradoxes of the Thatcherite administrations that they have successfully combined policies of active State intervention with the goal of increasing individual choice and responsibility and, therefore, constitute an example of the inadequacy of the State–market opposition on which ideologically they are based. When State intervention has been decreased, however, this has been done in such a way as to increase the freedom of capital rather than that of the consumer, largely at the expense of those with low incomes and in poor labour market positions, rather than to protect the weak and moderate the effects of the free market in capital. It would be a tragedy if those who are horrified at the effects of these policies failed to learn the Thatcherite lesson which gives the lie to Thatcherite ideology: that State intervention and individual freedom and choice are not opposed. They are only opposed if the State attempts to supplant the operation of markets rather than regulate or intervene in them. One purpose of State intervention is, rather, to make markets work better.

It must be recognized at this point that the State–market opposition is not the unique property of Thatcherites. Indeed, it may be argued that it is shared by many of those on the left who espouse the 'socialism' that Mrs Thatcher has sworn to destroy and who, like her, identify socialism with the public ownership of the means of production, distribution and exchange. Such socialism is, however, superficial, in that it fails to recognize that the core of socialism is a critique of capitalism which demonstrates that under capitalism, the satisfaction of human needs is given second place to the maximization of the rate of profit. Once *that* is firmly understood it becomes possible to be flexible and pragmatic about how the satisfaction of unmet human needs can best be achieved under any given set of historical circumstances. Thatcherism supposes that institutions are intrinsically bad; the left has traditionally supposed that institutions of State ownership are intrinsically good. Both views are misplaced. It is as great a mistake to suppose that any particular set of institutions is good or bad as it is to suppose that institutions as such are good or bad.

This returns us to the central place of institutions in social life and their character not as the opposites but as the constituents of markets. Institutions constitute markets in three senses. The first is obvious once we get away from economic abstraction. A market in commonsense terms is a place where people expect to be able to exchange goods for other goods or money. If there was no social agreement to exchange goods through some central 'place', exchanges would be restricted to exchanges between pairs of individuals who happened by chance to discover that they shared complementary interests. A great deal of attention has been given in the Thatcher years to improving the organization of the stock market, i.e. to improve the social institutions which make the buying and selling of stocks possible and hence create a market for them. According to the State-market philosophy this should not be necessary. Rather, rival stock exchanges should be established creating healthy competition which could stimulate the stock exchange to improve its efficiency. This is of course absurd, since the market for stocks becomes less efficient the more submarkets there are. Instead, the Government has encouraged institutional changes in the single institution; that is to say, the State has acted to improve the efficiency of a market. It has only been able to do so because of the crucial role of institutions in creating markets. Similarly, the establishment of Labour Exchanges in 1908 is an example of State intervention to improve the operation of the labour market. Institutions are not the opposite of markets but their precondition, and State intervention is not necessarily inimical to the operation of markets.

The second sense in which institutions constitute markets is equally banal. The market is not made up of individual buyers and sellers only. After the 1987 crash, everyone was waiting to see when 'the institutions' (e.g. the big pension funds) would start buying again. Equally, the biggest producers and consumers of goods and services are not individuals but corporate groups of one kind or another. Governments have traditionally intervened (the US anti-Trust legislation; the British Monopolies Commission) to prevent supply and demand of particular goods falling into the hands of a few large institutions. Once again, it is because markets are made up of institutions that the way is open for governments to intervene to make markets work better.

The third sense is more profound. The State–market dichotomy presents us with an image of social life in which there are two parts: a population of isolated individuals each pursuing their own private interests who are bound together through their submission to a common political authority. In Mrs Thatcher's terminology, the only sense in which 'Britain' is something more than 'individuals and their families' (the words she used in her *Woman's Own* interview), is that those individuals share common political institutions. However, that is an impossibility, since both State and market depend upon the existence of common beliefs, values, and practices over and above those constituting the State and market institutions themselves. More specifically, the practice of the exchange of commodities for profit arises out of the process of the production and reproduction of social life which is already constituted as such by a whole complex of institutionalized beliefs, relationships and practices possessed by a population which is thereby structured into categories and groups. There is nothing wrong with the attempt to make markets work better; there is everything wrong in attempting to do this by abolishing institutions instead of reforming them, i.e. trying to force social reality to approximate to an absurd theoretical abstraction.

The State and the market are not necessarily inimically opposed and the State can intervene to make markets work better. However, even the best of markets has its limitations. Thatcherite markets are the arenas for the unashamed pursuit of individual self-interest. Mrs Thatcher's polemics against 'wetness' signify a clear-eyed rejection of the view that you can improve society by improving individuals. Rather than appealing to the better instincts of the population, the nation's affairs must be so organized that the common good may be achieved by an appeal to people's baser instincts. Government must decide what needs to be done and provide the incentives which will motivate individuals to do it. If the State and other institutions did not intervene in markets they would work better, and the greatest good of the greatest number would be 'delivered' by the pursuit of individual self-interests.

This very ancient 'right' argument is deeply flawed. Markets are supposed to be more conducive to the common good the more 'free' they are. However, it is false to suppose that, once free, any market necessarily and 'naturally' moves towards a situation where market members face each other as isolated individual competitors. On the contrary, it is equally natural for market members with common interests to band together to protect those interests by reducing competition through the effecting of some sort of market closure. It is not merely the case that markets do not conform to the abstract ideal because they are structured by institutions, categories and groups which exist independently of them; the competitive practice of exchange itself leads to the formation of groups and the institutionalization of practices which moderate the rigour of competition. In other words, the pursuit of self-interest itself leads to the restriction of trade and a movement away from the pure market situation in which all members act as isolated individuals. Hence, any attempt by the State to eliminate such restrictions is an endless task, a task which cannot be achieved even in three terms of Thatcherite endeavour.

The point is so important that it is worth elaborating. Let it be granted that in contemporary Britain individuals in practice conform their behaviour to the model of economic rationality axiomatically assumed by neoclassical economics. Given this assumption there is no reason to suppose that individuals will optimize their economic welfare in such a way as to move the market of which they are a member closer towards the neoclassical ideal of perfection which constitutes the 'free market' criterion by which markets may be judged to work better. Even granted that if this were to happen it would be in the general interest, it does not follow that this would be in the interest of each member of the market. Indeed, it is in the interest of each to reduce the degree of competition, not increase it.

Clearly, from the free market standpoint, to restrict competition is wrong; that is to say, that there is a morality which is intrinsic to free market theory. From this it follows that the operation of the market system does not depend, after all, on the selfish pursuit of individual profit and interest, but on the moral regulation of this pursuit. Hence the successful pursuit of Thatcherite policies requires as well as the destruction of the old consensus the *imposition* of a new value consensus, which in turn requires the control of the media, the educational system and the silencing of moral dissent such as that currently expressed by the churches. But such an attempt involves the intervention by the State to regulate 'natural' market processes.

This takes us to a more profound contradiction in Thatcherism. Collective regulation of individual activity is conceived always as regulation by political institutions, and individual action as motivated by self-interest. This ignores the fact that individual action is also regulated by moral sentiments. Just as people do not obey the law simply because of fear of punishment, they do not work simply for monetary reward. They accept responsibility to others with whom they are related through their work, and take pride in what they do independently of the monetary reward for it. If they did not, if they acted at all times purely as greedy, acquisitive, selfish individuals, all cooperative activity in production would be impossible. Both cooperation and competition are essential features of human life. But whereas life can go on without competition (however inefficiently), production without cooperation is an impossibility. By emphasizing those Victorian values associated with competition

Mrs Thatcher risks eliminating the other values – duty, loyalty, diligence, responsibility – on which capitalism has equally depended for its success.

Beyond the opposition

The inadequacy of the State–market opposition, while giving Thatcherism the appearance of having made politics once again the art of the possible, has led it to embark upon an impossible task. It is at present a form of political practice which involves massive State intervention in social processes which is prevented from rationalizing that intervention by its own commitment to non-intervention. Thatcherism does not involve rolling back the frontiers of the State in this sense of the term. What it has done, however, is to destroy the identification of State intervention with State ownership, activity and control, and to recognize frankly the extent to which economic prosperity is dependent on the individual pursuit of material interests. That recognition emphasizes rather than obviates the need for State intervention. The chief political danger that it poses derives from its confusion of consumer with capital markets, which allows it to legitimize the removal of restraint on the freedom of capital on the grounds that this increases the freedom of the individual citizen.

Thatcherism has, however, dealt a massive blow to an increasingly sterile political tradition, which saw markets as intrinsically evil and the extension of State provision, activity and control as self-evidently superior. The way is now open to move away from these ancient simplicities as well as from those of Thatcherism and rethink the interventionist role of the State in a complex capitalist market economy. The role can now be seen not as *replacing* markets by the State but simultaneously increasing both market provision and State intervention to make markets work better. However, in devising policies of intervention, 'better' must not be understood in the New Right sense, which equates better with a movement towards the 'pure market' definition of classical economics. 'Better' means better in the sense of optimizing the satisfaction of consumer needs, rather than assuming that those needs are necessarily optimized by the market, and liberating, not capital, but people.

References

Ascher, K. (1987). *The Politics of Privatisation*. London: Macmillan.
Bulpitt, J. (1986). The discipline of the new democracy: Mrs Thatcher's domestic statecraft. *Political Studies*, **34**(1), 19–39.
Giner, S. (1976). *Mass Society*. London: Martin Robinson.
McInnes, J. (1987). *Thatcherism at Work*. Milton Keynes: Open University Press.
Smith, A. (1776). *The Wealth of Nations*. Oxford: Clarendon Press (reprinted 1987).

2 Unemployment

David N. Ashton

The policies of the New Right

The assumption of office by Mrs Thatcher coincided with the onset of recession. Saatchi and Saatchi's slogan, 'Labour isn't working', with its picture of an endless dole queue, was symptomatic of the belief among the New Right that the problem of unemployment could only be resolved by the Government stepping back and letting market forces operate freely. As Harris has shown, in the ideology of the New Right, market forces were seen as beneficial while State action or involvement was bad. In this respect, the success of the New Right in challenging the dominance of Keynesian economics had re-established the old argument of Adam Smith against that of the mercantilists that only if market forces were left free and unrestrained by the State could the wealth of the nation be increased. This time it was not the actions of the State in protecting the agrarian interests that was the focus of the struggle; rather the encroachment of the Socialist State and its attempts to control the market. It was this throttling of the market by the State which was seen as responsible for the two main economic and social problems facing Britain, namely inflation and the decline of the British economy in relation to its competitors. The task of the New Right was to destroy this collectivist heritage and so liberate market forces.

Following Gamble (1986), the New Right ideology can be seen to have three main components: the doctrine of economic individualism, libertarianism and Austrian economics. Economic individualism argues for the enlargement of the market in order to enhance the scope for individual choice. Libertarianism argues that only the minimal State can be justified, that which protects lives and property, while Austrian economics argues that there is no middle ground between capitalism and socialism. These three strands were united in the doctrine of monetarism.

Monetarists argued that inflation was caused by an excess of money in the economy. By attempting to reduce the level of unemployment in the economy by increasing the supply of money, previous governments had created a situation in which 'too much money was chasing too few goods'. Inflation was inevitable unless increases in the money supply were matched by increases in output. The cure for inflation was to reduce the money supply, which in practical terms meant reducing the level of State expenditure. This might cause unemployment in the short run until the relationship between output, employment and prices was stabilized and the 'natural' level of unemployment was reached. However, the achievement of this level could be hindered by institutional factors such as powerful unions, State agencies and welfare systems which interfered with the working of the market.

To cure inflation required policies which would redefine the relationship between the State and the economy. The State should restrict its activities to managing the maintenance of external defence, law and order and the administration of taxation. Apart from maintaining a sound money policy it should not interfere with the economy other than removing impediments to the effective operation of market forces. Once this was achieved, it would cure the unemployment problem and also enhance the discipline of the market on companies, exposing them to competition, and thereby ensuring a more productive and competitive industrial base which would reverse the industrial decline.

The moral basis of such a policy rested on the claim that it would enhance the scope for individual action and responsibility. By reducing the activities of the State, taxation could be reduced, thereby ensuring greater reward for individual effort. Constraints on the rights of individuals imposed by collectivities such as trade unions would be removed. Similarly, dependence on the State which was encouraged by generous social security payments would be reduced. By cutting benefits individuals would be encouraged to re-enter the labour market and fend for themselves.

The success of monetarists in the late 1970s in discrediting Keynesian demand management meant that at the ideological level there was no alternative when the first Thatcher administration came to power. A sound money policy had displaced full employment as the main policy objective. There could be no commitment to full employment. Indeed, all that monetarists could realistically expect was a return to the 'natural' level of unemployment and then only after the impediments to the free play of market forces had been removed.

The administration of unemployment policy

As the recession deepened when the Conservative administration took power in 1979, there was an initial belief that the increase in unemployment was just part of the normal business cycle. Once a sound money policy was established and the economy picked up again unemployment would be reduced. For this reason, the Government continued with the counter-cyclical measures initiated by the previous Labour Government. These were temporary job creation and work experience schemes aimed at those most severely affected by the recession – youths.

The first major problem for this policy occurred when the level of unemployment continued to rise between 1981 and 1983, when the economy was entering a period of business recovery. The Government found itself in an awkward position. Unemployment was not responding as it should according to the theory. As a result, a number of scapegoats were offered and the longer unemployment went on rising the greater the number of scapegoats that were offered. At first the rising level of unemployment was blamed on the previous government, but as it continued to rise it was argued that unemployment was the result of the international situation over which Britain had no control. Given the ideology of monetarism the only action the State could usefully take was to make the market work better by removing any impediments. This line of action fitted well with the broader political objectives of the New Right, to roll back the involvement of the State in the operation of the labour market and withdraw the legal and institutional supports which had previously been introduced to modify the imbalance in power relations between management and labour. Such a line of action would also restore management's right to manage.

The spotlight switched from one impediment to another. With regard to youth unemployment, initially the Government followed the lead of the Labour Party in arguing that it was the young people's fault that they were unemployed because they lacked the skills demanded by employers. However, as the level of youth unemployment continued to soar, that argument started to lose force as young people with good educational qualifications failed to secure work. The Government reacted quite pragmatically, abandoned non-intervention in the labour market and offered the Manpower Services Commission (MSC) funding for the training scheme for which the Commission had been arguing, provided that it catered for all young unemployed.

At the same time as this was happening the Government switched its emphasis onto a new cause of youth unemployment, high wages. This was now seen as the reason why the self-adjusting mechanisms inherent in the labour market were not reducing the problem. High wages were an institutional rigidity that had to be tackled: hence the attempt to lower wages by pitching the level of the new Youth Training Scheme (YTS) allowance just above that of supplementary benefits. This policy was reinforced by a series of subsidies for employers aimed at encouraging them to lower youth rates of pay.

The idea of institutional rigidities preventing the fall of unemployment as the recession bottomed out, was an appealing one. It was used to reduce the powers of the Wages Councils, legal protection of workers' rights and to justify further attacks on the powers of trade unions.

Meanwhile, the economy started to witness a new phenomenon, jobless growth. First, output began to increase but job losses continued in manufacturing; new jobs were created and the rate of job creation started to outstrip job losses, but registered unemployment failed to respond. Eventually the rate of new job creation accelerated sufficiently for the unemployment level to fall. However, many of the new jobs were part-time jobs in the service sector. Talk of institutional rigidities started to fall off, monetarism as a doctrine was no longer espoused, the 1987 election was approaching and money was pumped into the economy leading to a more sustained fall in the level of unemployment.

Once the market impediments had been cleared, the emphasis within the ideology of the New Right on individual responsibility meant that the way was open for individuals to be held responsible for the situation they found themselves in. This was done by reference to the traditional myth of the idle poor. The unemployed were responsible for their own plight. This strategy was made famous by Norman Tebbit's call for the unemployed to 'get on their bikes'. The continuous propagation of this theme also provided the legitimation for a further course of action which was to tighten up on the welfare benefits available. As the numbers of unemployed increased, attempts were made to contain the costs, producing savings estimated at £540 million.[1] This was achieved by a constant tightening of benefits.

A further course of action was to change the public perception of the problem by reducing the numbers recorded as unemployed. By 1988 a series of 17 changes had been made of which only one led to an increase in the numbers on the register. Were the pre-1982 definitions applied in May 1988, the number of unemployed would have been 3,123,100 as opposed to the official figure of 2,429,900.[2]

Over the period 1979–88, the Government steadfastly refused to raise the importance of unemployment in its hierarchy of values. The response was to deny consistently that there was anything the Government could do, apart from attempting to improve the operations of the market. At the same time, its other policies, on the exchange rate, industrial relations and the financing of the public sector, fuelled the rise in the level of unemployment. The refusal to act directly to raise levels of employment was an integral part of the overall strategy to solve the country's economic problem by restricting State finances, and by helping the market to become more responsive to fluctuations in supply and demand. Unemployment was the cost that society had to bear in order that free market forces could solve the country's economic problems.

The recession and economic change

The initial consequences of the recession were predictable on the basis of our knowledge of previous recessions. The fall in demand caused employers to cut back on labour costs. The easiest way to do this was to stop recruitment, a policy advocated by unions as a means of protecting the jobs of existing members. The result was a disproportionate increase in unemployment among young people. In addition, employers encouraged older workers to leave, using redundancy payments and early retirement plans to ease the transition. This was a prospect fairly readily taken up by many workers, as they expected on the basis of previous experience to be able to move into another job. As the recession deepened, the existing long-term unemployed found it more difficult to re-enter paid work. However, by 1983–4 it was becoming clear that there were a number of features about this recession that differed from those of the past (for a detailed discussion, see Ashton *et al.*, 1989).

First, employment in manufacturing industry did not pick up as would have been expected. As output bottomed out and slowly started to increase, employment in manufacturing continued to fall. Moreover, the jobs that were being lost were not just those of the unskilled and semi-skilled who traditionally fare worst in a recession, but included the skilled craftworkers. While this was occurring, the proportion of more highly skilled professional, managerial and scientific workers continued to increase. However, the majority of new jobs were predominantly part-time jobs, many of which were filled by married women who had not been registered as unemployed. For a short time this produced a situation of job growth and increasing unemployment. All this was indicative of structural changes taking place in the economy of which the Government was only dimly aware.

There were three major processes of change at work which contributed to this restructuring of the labour market. These were the extension of global markets, industrial concentration and the introduction of new technology. The restructuring they caused not only contributed towards mass unemployment and its persistence through time, but also changed the conditions of life of a large section of the working class.

Perhaps the most significant of the three was the change taking place in the structure of competition in product markets, involving as it did the incorporation of British firms into global markets. Firms which had traditionally enjoyed an oligarchical position in British markets found themselves threatened by the encroachment of foreign firms into their markets. Competition from firms in the USA, Europe and the new industrial countries intensified. Firms which had previously enjoyed a dominant position in the British market now found themselves struggling to survive as relatively small units in a much larger and more competitive global market. Perhaps of even greater significance, the Japanese had entered many product markets with organizations capable of achieving much higher levels of productivity than British firms had ever achieved.

In the face of competition from low labour-cost countries some of the larger firms withdrew from manufacturing labour-intensive products. As a result, capital for such industries was relocated. This accelerated the loss of jobs in textiles, footwear and clothing. In the engineering industry, many firms went bankrupt or were absorbed by others. Where British-based firms survived, they were having to adapt to changed product market conditions and attempt to match Japanese levels of labour productivity. To do this, some were just intensifying the existing use of labour, but others were introducing new technology together with new labour force management strategies. The effect of the new technology was a radical change in the amount of labour required to achieve a given level of production, a process of change which was cutting out many of the traditional craft jobs in engineering. Changes in labour management strategies were aimed at breaking the occupational-based shelters of the traditional crafts, and creating a more flexible labour force. Of course, these changes were not confined to the period 1979–87; many of them were longer-term changes which preceded the recession. However, the recession accelerated them by putting British firms at a disadvantage through adverse trading conditions associated with over-valued sterling.

It was these changes which were producing the more competitive environment facing British firms. The discipline of the market was stemming not so much from the enlargement of the market within Britain as from wider changes in the international division of labour. The contribution of the Government was to insist that all industries should stand or fall alone in meeting this challenge. There was to be no help from the State in 'propping up lame ducks', as this smacked of the kind of socialist intervention that they were struggling to eradicate. For them, only the market could provide the solution, and in that market only the fittest would survive. British firms were to be given no preference and no impediments should be placed in the way of the free movement of capital.

The result was a substantial decline in manufacturing capacity and a massive loss of jobs. The process of restructuring was aided further by shifts in the balance of power which the Government's policy of labour market deregulation had achieved. As one firm after another closed and others made workers redundant, the power of the unions to resist was undermined. In the engineering industry alone, over 1 million jobs were lost between 1979 and 1984, almost all of them full-time and many of them skilled manual jobs. As firms started to turn around and expand output, this was achieved by a combination of new technology, new manning levels and the reallocation of tasks.

In the service sector the situation was very different. There the product market, which was largely domestic, continued to grow, but the labour market was also subject to radical change. This was due to the increasing industrial concentration taking place in that sector. The most dramatic effect of this was seen in the hotel, catering and retail trades. There the traditional unit of operation had been the family business employing workers (mostly women) on a full-time basis. However, these smaller units were becoming increasingly dominated by, or incorporated into, new, rapidly growing, capital-intensive, national corporations. The superiority of these organizations in competitive terms lay not just in their massive purchasing power and control over manufacturers, but also in the way in which they could reduce labour costs. On taking over a smaller business, for example in hotels and catering, labour was rationalized; the precise labour requirements of the service were established and full-time workers who experienced periods of slack were replaced by part-timers who were called in to cover for periods of peak demand. As these organizations displaced remaining family businesses, and as the demand for services grew, so the new jobs created were part-time, designed often deliberately to appeal to married women. Thus, the recession witnessed a major growth of part-time work. As many of the women who filled these jobs were not on the unemployment register, there existed the apparent contradiction of increasing unemployment together with an increasing number of new jobs.

Although dimly aware of these changes, the Government facilitated them and enhanced their impact on job losses by a series of political actions aimed at the destruction of some forms of market shelter, previously established to safeguard jobs. A number of different tactics were used to achieve this goal. One was to make strategic appointments to leadership positions within the nationalized industries. Thus, in the steel and coal industries, Ian MacGregor was brought in to rationalize the industries, to reduce the power of the unions and reorganize production to achieve higher levels of productivity. A second tactic was legislative changes which reduced employees' protection against dismissal, and weakened the measures unions could take in the pursuit of industrial disputes. The third was through the policy of privatizing services. All these actions tended to increase the magnitude of job losses created by the underlying processes of change.

The Government's obsession with monetarist policies during the early 1980s prevented it from recognizing and mitigating the effects of these underlying changes. By sustaining a high exchange rate, manufacturers who were facing a painful process of readjustment found their task even harder. The deregulation of the market helped them in the process of restructuring their labour forces, but only under adversarial conditions. In the service sector, where unions and the institutional regulation of the labour market was weak, the policy of deregulation was largely irrelevant. The result was that the process of industrial and labour-market restructuring was made substantially worse for labour in Britain than in most other advanced industrial societies.

The consequence for the unemployed in Britain was that they became caught in a trap. The jobs that had been lost were full-time jobs, often skilled and filled by males. The new jobs, when they came in large numbers, were either very highly skilled, for professionals, scientists or managers, or more frequently part-time jobs for which employers were seeking married women or youths. For the bulk of the unemployed who were establishing or maintaining a household, such jobs offered no way out.

For some workers, the combination of the new labour-force management strategies and government measures did provide occasional respites from unemployment. This came in the form of short-term jobs or government schemes, but precisely because of their short-term character this meant that many would become unemployed once the job or scheme was completed. The ensuing history of a short-term or casual job followed by unemployment, followed by another casual job or government scheme was not unknown before the recession (Norris, 1978). What was new, was the rapid expansion of this phenomenon during the recession and its incursion into parts of the labour market which had previously been the province of secure, stable, skilled occupations which had provided the basis of the traditional working class.

Another major feature of the unemployment problem was the spatial one. Traditional manufacturing industries predominated in the Midlands, the North and inner cities and these areas experienced the worst effects of unemployment. The newer, high-technology industries were increasingly in the South, together with the headquarters of major corporations and, consequently, the business service industries were also located there. The division between the two parts of Britain, the affluent South-East and the more deprived areas of the Midlands, North and South-West widened and long-term unemployment became highly concentrated.

According to official figures, the long-term unemployed numbered 1,029,206 in April 1988. But the magnitude of the problem becomes more evident when it is realized that in the region of 900,000 children under 19 were growing up in the families of the long-term unemployed. These were the workers who, having become trapped in a situation of unemployment when structural changes were taking place in the demand for labour, now found themselves unable to secure even casual or temporary work.

The mechanics of the exclusion process are fairly clear. These are workers who are either unskilled or are skilled workers caught in a dying industry. In the major cities, they are typically living in council housing and concentrated in certain parts of the city. As the level of unemployment rises employers find it sufficient to 'put the word out' in order to recruit workers. Those within the plant or office pass on the message and relatives or friends appear for the job. However, as more and more members of a particular community or estate become unemployed the community loses access to those information networks. The unemployed become excluded from the labour market.

Given the length of time some members of such communities have been without work, we now face a situation of second-generation unemployment, and there is evidence from this group that unemployment is being socially inherited (Payne, 1987; Ashton and Maguire, 1986). Given the exclusion of the long-term unemployed from the job information networks it follows that their children will also become excluded. Hence the higher rates of unemployment among the second generation, a generation who are now starting to raise their own families without ever having had any experience of work.

There is no evidence that this group have in any sense lost the desire for work, which if it were available would provide them with an escape from the poverty which they are forced to endure. However, constant deprivation does alter attitudes to petty crime and delinquency. If food or clothes are available cheaply no one asks questions. If the chance of earning a little additional money is made available, then its acceptance as a 'fiddle' job, undeclared to the authorities, is automatic. However, the fear of being 'shopped' is a constant worry and these communities become apprehensive of outsiders and suspicious of each other. (For a more detailed discussion of the evidence on the effects of unemployment, see Ashton, 1986).

Life on the dole is not a pleasant experience. Poverty pervades all aspects of life. The lack of financial resources means that collective security, providing for the rent and ensuring that there is minimal warmth and food, are the priorities and constitute problems which have to be faced week in and week out. Clothes come as hand-me-downs, from jumble sales or 'off the back of lorries'. Social life is restricted as resources limit the range of social activities. In the absence of work, time becomes a problem, because alternative ways of structuring it have to be devised. Illness is more prevalent among such communities and the risk of mortality increases as does that of suicide. Mental health suffers as the stress of daily living increases.

These then are some of the costs of unemployment to those who carry most of them. Others are carried by the sub-employed who struggle to maintain a toe-hold in the labour market and access to resources that will keep them above the poverty line. Politically, neither of these two groups constitute a threat in the short term. The sense of alienation and exclusion leads to a sense of fatalism and disbelief in political solutions. However, there is a cost to society apart from the obvious loss of wealth-creating capacity, and that is the threat of crime, delinquency, drug abuse, etc. Society carries a considerable cost in the form of extra policing, periodic outbursts of violence, the establishment of virtual no-go areas in parts of the cities, and the gradual erosion of the quality of life associated with more highly integrated societies. These then are just some of the costs of a policy which regards high levels of unemployment as a necessary condition to help ensure the establishment of a free market economy unfettered by any institutional rigidities or constraints.

Towards an alternative to Thatcherism

One of the achievements of Thatcherism has been to place the question of the creation of wealth at the centre of the political agenda. In achieving this the power of the State apparatus has been used to reshape the structure of the market, providing fewer constraints on the power of capital and making the provision of goods and services more responsive to the needs of consumers. As Harris argues in Chapter 1, it has destroyed the identification of State intervention with State ownership, activity and control, and has demonstrated the role of private material interest in economic growth. However, as an ideology it is still locked into the social and political conflicts of the nineteenth century, as it seeks to create a society in which the State, apart from its functions in ensuring law, order and defence, leaves the provision of goods and services to the free play of market forces. In fact, this was never the case even in the nineteenth century. In the late twentieth century after 10 years of the application of this doctrine, State activities remain central to the provision of health, education and welfare, and overall taxation levels have not fallen for the majority of people. State intervention remains: only its form has changed.

The major source of change has not been in the extent of State intervention, but in the international context in which the State operates. The British economy is no longer the 'Workshop of the World'.

It is now part of an infinitely larger and more highly integrated world economy in which it contributes only a small fraction of the total output of goods and services. It is now facing increasing competition from countries such as Singapore and Hong Kong, creations of its own colonial past, as well as Japan, the USA, Italy and the older industrial countries. In this context, an ideology forged in the struggle to 'free internal markets' in the nineteenth century, and which is now used to relive the old struggle between capital and labour, is totally inappropriate. It directs attention away from the important changes which are taking place in relationships between societies. However, by showing how the State can influence and shape the market and the distribution of goods and services without resorting to administration through large bureaucratic organizations, the concrete achievements of Thatcherism point the way forward.

The task now is to explore ways in which the State apparatus can be used to shape the economy and create a manufacturing base which is capable of competing effectively in world markets, while at the same time ensuring that the needs of the labour force are met through effective forms of provision. In the context of the labour market, this means not only the provision of more jobs but of jobs which facilitate rather than inhibit human growth. Here we can learn important lessons from other societies. These are societies which, because they have had to struggle to enter world markets as late starters, have succeeded in forging new relationships between the State and the economy.[3]

Unemployment: lessons from abroad

Despite the protestations of the New Right that there was 'no alternative', there were a number of societies in which the rate of unemployment did not rise significantly during the world recession. Most notable among these were Japan, Sweden, Norway and Switzerland. It could be argued that these were exceptional. Japan is unique in terms of its culture and economic performance, leading the capitalist world in terms of its productive capacity. In any case, observers point to the fact that unemployment is concealed by the life-time employment system, and the Japanese system of recording unemployment. In Sweden too, the use of labour market policy created make-work schemes which, it has been estimated, accounted for 6% of the labour force. Norway used similar tactics and was cushioned by North Sea oil. Finally, Switzerland merely exported the problem by sending its guest workers home. The only 'real' solution is economic growth and hence the creation of real jobs.

These observations raise two major points. The first is that the relationship between economic growth and full employment is a tenuous one. Therborn (1986) found that economic growth accounted for only

14% of the variation in unemployment increase among the 15 advanced OECD countries for which comparable data was available. Thus the experience of these 15 countries confirms the recent experience of Britain, namely that we cannot rely on economic growth alone to solve the problems of unemployment.

One of the ways in which Sweden and Norway achieved near full employment throughout the recession was through the use of labour-market policy to sustain employment in the form of training and job creation schemes. Indeed, Britain did the same, through the YTS and the Community Programme (CP), but such schemes were not adopted on any large scale. The Swedes currently spend four times more relative to their Gross National Product (GNP) than the British on employment services and adult training (O'Brien, 1988). They used the schemes to cushion the adjustment problems which their economies encountered, but more importantly than this, these governments had a commitment to full employment. They used the time available to the unemployed constructively, seeing it as an opportunity to retrain. Of course such schemes are expensive, but so is the alternative – long-term unemployment. In fact, when total spending on employment, training, welfare benefits and lost taxes due to unemployment is included, the Swedes spend less than the British. The commitment to full employment works out cheaper. Similiar calculations have shown that this would also be the case in Canada (Sub-Committee on Training and Employment, 1987).

In addition, such schemes can, if they provide an adequate income, avoid the negative consequences of unemployment on local communities and individuals. Like any other job they provide a regular income, a structure to time and a set of meaningful activities through which the individual makes a contribution to society. In Britain, as in other European societies, this strategy has been adopted in relation to school leavers. In effect, the YTS now takes young people off the labour market for 2 years. As the Swedes have shown, there is no reason why this period could not be further extended or why similar schemes could not be developed for adults, but the scale has to go far beyond that envisaged in current schemes.

Another characteristic of societies which have maintained full employment is their development of an active industrial strategy or enterprise-intervention strategy, as it is sometimes called. These were late developers or more accurately late follower countries (Laxer, 1987), where the ideology of the free market, which finds its extreme form in that of the New Right, never fully took hold. In such societies, the power of the bourgeoisie was tempered by the political influence of other social classes and industrialization was achieved by the State using its resources to co-ordinate market forces so that the country could not only catch up, but compete effectively in world markets. Industrial development was targeted in those areas where technology could be adapted to provide an industrial advantage. Thus, Japan originally targeted cars and electrical consumer goods, Sweden shipbuilding and engineering. Both societies have now moved into other areas. Such a policy has enabled these societies to compete more effectively in world markets than Britain, leaving them less at the mercy of changes in market forces. Where this policy has not been followed, and development left to market forces, as in countries such as Canada, the result has been a small manufacturing base owned in a large part by foreign investors – a prospect which now faces Britain.

Solutions for Britain

Britain's problems require the development of an ideology which offers the prospect of a partnership between the State, capital and labour, on the basis of which a competitive industrial framework can be forged. But more than the monetary needs of the population need to be met. The central concern should be to secure work which enhances rather than debases the human personality. Within such a framework, the State should supervise and take responsibility for ensuring that all the needs of its citizens are met, not just those which can conveniently be met through the operation of capital markets. Only in this way can we hope to achieve a sufficient level of integration within society to enable us to compete effectively with other countries while at the same time avoiding the level of violence, fear and poverty which characterize contemporary Britain. The development of such an ideology takes us beyond the scope of this chapter; all that is offered here are some suggestions about the direction of future policy.

First, as a trading nation exposed to the vagaries of world markets, it is important that policies aimed at stabilizing world trade are pursued. After the collapse of American dominance of world finance, new arrangements aimed at the international regulation of trade and finance should be encouraged to provide the institutional context within which world trade can grow.

Secondly, a commitment to full employment requires as an integral component a policy aimed at creating jobs. In Britain, such a policy needs to recognize the country's distinctive position in the context of the global markets which are now emerging. Britain has not been a dominant influence in world trade for some time. Having lost industrial leadership at the end of the nineteenth century, it is now a relatively small operation on the world stage. Once this nettle is grasped, the absurdity of trying to compete in all the various product markets becomes obvious. If we are to catch up and establish a strong presence we need to target those industries where we can achieve a positive advantage and develop policies that can ensure we have the firms capable of holding their own. In the context of the new global markets, this becomes even more urgent. Left to their own devices, the transnational companies, such as Ford and Nissan, will play one country off against another when deciding on the location of manufacturing plants, making individual governments bid to attract their investment and jobs.

Thirdly, the development of strong indigenous British and European companies capable of competing effectively in the growth markets is essential if the State is to retain any control over the types of jobs that are created and the quality of life with which they are associated. In view of the structural changes we identified above and the growth of short-term, casual and part-time employment, this concern with the types of jobs created needs to be placed in the centre of any policy which aims to sustain not just full employment, but full employment in the context of a society which creates meaningful employment for its members.

In this respect, the initial impact of global markets on the British economy provides some useful pointers with regard for employment policy and the types of companies and jobs to be encouraged. In engineering, those companies and jobs which have survived in world markets are those which have a strong knowledge base. In the labour-intensive industries, the large companies which survived have established market niches based on a strong Research and Development component. At the other end of the spectrum, the small companies which have competed successfully against cheaper imports from labour-intensive manufacturers in the low labour-cost countries have only done so by replicating the conditions of labour to be found in those countries. The service sector has seen the growth of professional and scientific occupations in finance and commerce, and to a lesser extent in retail, hotels and leisure, but the majority of jobs there are of the semi-skilled and unskilled part-time, low-paid variety. Across that spectrum, it is clear where, given a choice, resources need to be directed, namely towards the knowledge-based, full-time, well-paid occupations.

To maximize the number of such jobs means targeting those industries capable of providing them. The realities of global markets must be recognized and some institutional structures amended in order that companies can compete effectively. For example, the level of education in the population will need to be raised to ensure that the labour force can support knowledge-based industries. Painful adjustments will be necessary to trade unions, professional organizations and training practices, as well as the sacrifice of jobs in those industries where our ability to compete is in question, or where the quality of the jobs is such that we would not wish to encourage them.

Fourthly, as economic growth will not necessarily ensure full employment, such a policy has to be complemented by a labour market policy. This would have the aims of ensuring adequate training, facilitating the geographical mobility of labour and providing meaningful employment for those displaced by the process of adjustment. The training policy would need to ensure that training was available on a continuous basis for those wishing to upgrade or change skills. The policy on labour mobility would likewise provide aid for those who are severely disadvantaged in attempts to move to areas of labour demand.

The labour market policy would need to be more extensive and imaginative than that already on offer. It would need to produce high-quality training; the economic need is for highly trained workers, not more semi-skilled operatives or service workers. The fact that the Swedes spend £15,000 per trainee per year, the cost of an engineering student at a British university, compared with the projected £5000 envisaged in the new Training for Employment policy in Britain, is some measure of our current failure.

The labour market policy would also need to include programmes of job creation on a scale large enough to combat the forces which are excluding the long-term unemployed from participating in the labour market. These need not necessarily be administered by a large bureaucracy. They could take the form of grants available for groups of workers to develop their own activities such as housing cooperatives and community services, or individual programmes such as the more traditional job creation schemes, where work is provided by the State, which could be made available for those who felt more secure in such an environment. However, self-initiated projects offer far greater potential in extending the personal skills of the people involved. Such a variety of approaches would combat the negative effects of unemployment on the individuals concerned and the transmission of a culture of unemployment and State dependence from one generation to the next. It could also be expanded and contracted in accordance with changes in the private sector labour market.

In summary, it is argued that full employment is a practicable, realizable goal which has been successfully attained by a number of societies. It requires a commitment to an extensive and active labour market policy which goes way beyond that currently on offer. We have also argued for a policy which puts employment creation and a concern for the quality of working life at the centre of our economic strategy. Such a policy, while perfectly realizable, would need to be adapted to the realities of the new world markets if it is to enable us to regain some control over not only the number of jobs we create but also the quality of life they offer.

Notes

1 These figures are derived from the work Layard reported in the *Financial Times*, 16 May 1988.
2 These calculations are based on the work of the Unemployment Unit in London.
3 James Laxer (1987) provides an analysis of the strategies adopted by those countries who are succeeding in combining private competition with State intervention.

References

Ashton, D.N. (1986). *Unemployment under Capitalism*. Brighton: Wheatsheaf.

Ashton, D.N. and Maguire, M.J. (1986). *Young Adults in the Labour Market*. Research Paper No. 55. London: Department of Employment.

Ashton, D.N., Maguire, M.J. and Spilsbury, M. (1989). *Restructuring the Youth Labour Market: The Implications for Youth*. London: Macmillan.

Gamble, A. (1986). The political economy of freedom. In *The Ideology of the New Right* (R. Levitas, ed.) Cambridge: Polity Press.

Laxer, J. (1987). *Decline of the Super Powers: Winners and Losers in Today's Global Economy*. Toronto: Lorimer.

Norris, G.M. (1978). Unemployment, subemployment and personal characteristics. *Sociological Review*, 26, 327–47.

O'Brien, R. (1988). Swedes show how to save money by spending it. *Financial Times*, 4 May.

Payne, J. (1987). Does unemployment run in families? Some findings of the General Household Survey. *Sociology*, 21(2), 199–214.

Sub-Committee on Training and Employment of the Standing Senate Committee on Social Affairs, Science and Technology (1987). *In Training: Only Work Works*. Report. Ottawa: Canadian Government.

Therborn, G. (1986). *Why Some People are More Unemployed than Others*. London: Verso.

3 Education

Phillip Brown

In Mrs Thatcher's third term of office the educational system has been identified as being in need of a dose of Thatcherism. Indeed she has recently stated that 'we are going much further with education than we had ever thought of going before' (Simon, 1988). This radical shift in educational policy is manifest in the Education Reform Bill (HMSO, 1987) which is intended to offer parents more choice and variety of schools in order to improve educational opportunities and standards for all. Moreover, the Secretary of State for Education, Kenneth Baker (1987), has noted that:

> Education can no longer be led by the producers – the academic theorists, the administrators, and even the teachers' unions.... Education must be shaped by the users – by what is good for the individual child and what hopes are held by parents.

The reason for this change in educational provision stems from a belief that our schools are in crisis, which is the result of the educational system being organized to serve the ideological and vested interests of the providers rather than those of the consumers (i.e. parents, employers), whose interests are presumed to be more in tune with the 'national' interest. However, anything other than the most superficial examination reveals that the educational agenda is not being set as a result of parental demands for more participation or 'choice'[1] but, as Kenneth Baker was overheard telling his political advisor in the House of Lords, by a small group of New Right intellectuals who are members of the Centre for Policy Studies (Wilby and Midgley, 1987).

The purpose of this chapter is to locate the 'Thatcher revolution' in education in the context of the right's attack on comprehensive education, which dates back to the publication of the first Black Paper (Cox and Dyson, 1968). I will show that the ideas of the right are having a major impact on current educational legislation. Nor do their demands end with the Education Reform Bill. Further changes such as the introduction of educational vouchers may become a reality. It will also be shown, that although their attack on comprehensive education is couched in terms of an apolitical concern about declining educational and moral standards, their explanations and remedies are based on unsubstantiated assertions and often contradictory and inconsistent ideological dogma. Nevertheless, their ideas provide the foundation for a major educational experiment. This involves a move away from a form of education organized on the basis of 'age, aptitude and ability', as enshrined in the 1944 Education Act, to one in which the education a child receives must conform to the *wealth and wishes of parents*; that is, from the ideology of *meritocracy* (Young, 1961) to what I will call the ideology of *parentocracy*. In conclusion, I will sketch some of the main elements of an alternative popular politics of education.

Crisis, what crisis?

During the 1970s there was a growing consensus that the educational system was in crisis due to the failure of comprehensive schools to meet either of the twin objectives which helped to bring them into being. They were seen neither to have led to a significant improvement in working-class educational and occupational mobility, nor to have significantly contributed to greater economic expansion or efficiency. The radical right's account of the educational crisis during this period (see Cox and Dyson, 1968; Cox and Boyson, 1977) took the argument a stage further by asserting that the comprehensive experiment had not only failed, but was the cause of declining educational standards. They argued that the spirit of competition and excellence had been sacrificed in order to make the educational system conform to a socialist notion of social justice,[2] and that there is therefore a need to defend merit, standards and achievement against those who promote mediocrity in the name of social justice:

> It must always be remembered that the deterioration in British education has arisen partly because schools have been treated as instruments for equalizing, rather than instructing, children. Merit, competition and self-esteem have been devalued or repudiated; the teaching of facts has given way to the inculcation of opinion; education has often been confounded with indoctrination; and in many places there is a serious risk of disciplined study being

entirely swamped by an amorphous tide of easy-going discussion and idle play (Hillgate Group, 1987:2).

The right's critique of the current crisis chooses to ignore the fact that the 'academic' grammar school curriculum continues to dominate the content of comprehensive education; that the use of streaming and the banding of pupils makes those attempts at mixed-ability teaching pale into insignificance; and that the orientation towards examination success remains sacrosanct. Nevertheless, the right invariably present the shift to comprehensive education as a radical transformation, which Flew (1987) has compared with the Bolshevik Revolution in 1917:

> This truly radical reorganisation has sometimes been described as a great experiment; just as, in the 1920s and the 1930s, the operations of the regime established by the Bolshevik coup of October 1917 were regularly characterised as 'that great social experiment in Russia'.
> Certainly, the continuing effects of the Comprehensive Revolution are both very extensive and extremely important (Flew, 1987:24)[3]

The difficulty faced by the right in their attempt to impute a socialist revolutionary character to the shift towards comprehensive education is, of course, the participation of post-war Conservative governments in the reform of selective education.

Such difficulties, however, do not affect the contention that the comprehensive experiment has failed. Indeed, because of the hopelessly optimistic belief that comprehensive education could overcome broader social inequalities and Britain's economic troubles, the proponents of liberal democratic reforms have found it difficult to argue against the right's critique. The right have argued that the comprehensive experiment has not only failed the working class, but betrayed it. They assert that comprehensive reorganization has both eroded the standards of our élite schools because of their contamination by the masses, and led the masses to receive an education which is not suited to their 'needs' (see Bantock, 1977); therefore, a decline in educational standards is assumed to be inevitable.

The issue of declining educational standards has been at the heart of the right's attack on comprehensive education for many years (Cox and Dyson, 1968). However, objective evidence of declining standards is difficult to come by. Wright, for example, has noted that 'in 558 pages of Black Papers so far published, not one piece of sound evidence has been produced to show that standards are declining' (Wright, 1983:175), and the same can be said of more recent claims about declining educational standards (see McPherson and Willms, 1987; Simon, 1988; Goldstein and Cuttance, in press).

At least Flew (1987) is willing to admit that it is very difficult to measure standards particularly in terms of literacy and numeracy. He does, however, try to offer some evidence of problems of numeracy on the basis of comparative data, but this can hardly be used to prove that there has been a decline in educational standards, only that we need improvements. But even if standards could be shown to have declined (or more plausibly not to have significantly improved), it is mistaken to assume that this is due, either wholly or in part, to comprehensive reorganization. Schooling does not take place in a social, economic or political vacuum. The circumstances of the 1980s are considerably different from those in the 1950s and 1960s, because, among other things, our schools were better funded and teacher morale was much higher then than today. Moreover, the vast majority of school leavers got jobs, which research has shown to be an important motivator. The virtual collapse of job opportunities for some school leavers in the 1980s (DES, 1987) has led many of them to ask whether it remains worth 'making an effort' in school (Brown, 1987). Despite these cuts in government expenditure and the changing context outside the school, it is not difficult to find evidence which suggests that against all the odds educational standards may actually be rising (see Simon, 1988). Recent evidence has also shown that comprehensive education may well be benefiting pupils from a working-class background (McPherson and Willms, 1987).

The lack of credible evidence to support the assertion that educational standards have declined, let alone to show that any decline is the result of comprehensive reorganization, has not prevented the question of 'standards' from remaining at the centre of what the right define as the educational crisis. This is because 'standards' are as much a moral as an educational issue. The main concern of the authoritarian right is to regain traditional authority, leadership and the reproduction of élite culture, in which the educational system is seen to have a key role to play. For them, *it is the very idea of comprehensive education which violates their notion of standards, not only its imputed consequences.* It is the shift from élite to mass culture, and the erosion of respect for authority which they oppose. This desire often contradicts the goals of the Thatcherite 'free marketeers' whose ideas derive from classical liberalism (see Belsey, 1986; Scruton, 1984). Here emphasis is placed on the 'free market economy' and 'individual liberty'. An uneasy alliance between the authoritarian conservatives and the 'market' men and women has been possible due to their mutual disdain of 'collective social reform'. Classical liberals oppose such reforms because they 'consider them to be menaces to freedom, conservatives, because they consider them to be equalitarian in tendency' (Phillips, 1978:12).

The potential conflict among the right has so far been limited because despite their ideological differences both serve the political and material interests of the powerful and privileged. In a free market society, although we may have formal equality before the law, we do not have substantive equality. Moreover, the privatization of education has an appeal to the authoritarian conservatives, because the latter believe that if left to the free market, not only would the traditional schools be preserved, but also the schooling for different social groups would 'diversify as society required' (Scruton, 1984:160). Yet, despite the rhetoric of 'freedom' and 'parental choice', Thatcherism clearly asserts that education is not only too important to be left to teachers, but is also too important to be left to the 'free market'.

The Thatcher Government is attempting to centralize control over education which traditionally has been organized locally under the guidance of the Department of Education and Science (DES). Justification for the centralization of educational power is based on the contention that the local education authorities (LEAs) are largely responsible for the current educational crisis, despite the fact that the Black Papers did not see a major reduction in the power of the LEAs as a route to higher educational standards. There is no escaping the fact that the recent right-wing attacks on the LEAs (Hillgate Group, 1986) are motivated by the wider political concerns to break the power of Labour-controlled local authorities, and have little to do with improving the quality of education (see Simon, 1988). It is now received wisdom among the right and the tabloid press, that LEAs and the teachers' unions are more interested in peddling left-wing propaganda than raising educational standards.[4] Evidence advanced for this includes the existence of anti-racist and anti-sexist policies, and the teaching of peace studies and sex education (especially in inner-London schools). The solution to this crisis is seen to require nothing less than the centralization of educational control as well as the demolition of comprehensive education.

The right's reform of education

The centrepiece of the right's educational policy is the establishment of an 'independent education for all' (Flew, 1987; Hillgate Group, 1987). This would mean that the LEAs would no longer be the main providers of 'education' and the comprehensive system would be scrapped. In order to establish an 'independent education for all', it is necessary to think of schools as separate educational firms, subject like the presently existing independent schools to the incentives and discipline of the market. It is argued that a major advantage of this kind of educational arrangement is that it maximizes variety and choice, while rejecting all attempts to impose and sustain what its proponents see as a state 'monopoly' and a 'uniform service' for all its consumers. Hence, two conditions need to exist in order to achieve an 'independent education for all'. First, all parents should be free and able to move their children from one school to another if they so desire and, secondly, that every school should have strong financial incentives to attract and to hold custom, and have sufficient reason to fear disaster if it fails (Flew, 1987). This system of *survival by results* involves the privatisation of education:

> The aim ... is to offer an independent education to all, by granting to all parents the power, at present enjoyed only by the wealthy, to choose the best available education for their children. This aim can be accomplished only by offering schools the opportunity to liberate themselves from Local Authority control (Hillgate Group, 1987:2).

If parents want to buy their children a private education it is entirely up to them, because education, like a video-recorder or a dishwasher, is regarded as a commodity. Therefore, any fetter to the supply and demand for education should be removed because it is assumed that open competition between schools will raise standards for all and offer real choices to parents. However, those schools which fail to recruit enough pupils (sell desk space for the services they have on offer) should be allowed to go out of business.

The idea of an 'independent education for all' could be dismissed as extremist nonsense were it not for the fact that these views are shaping the future direction of British education (see Lauder, 1987; Shor, 1986). Already the Educational Reform Bill,[5] which includes the financial delegation to schools, open enrolement, charging for school activities and opting out (grant-maintained schools), is the first step towards educational privatization and the establishment of an 'independent education for all'. The most important features of the Bill in terms of the structure of the education system are 'open enrolment' and 'opting out'. The former is particularly damaging to the planning of local educational systems because the secondary school population is declining and the number of pupils which any school can admit is to be set at the 1979 level. This was a year when the school population was much higher than it is now. The Government has argued that open enrolment is necessary to give parents more 'choice' of school. This remains to be seen, but the prospect of chaos and school closures seems to be inevitable. The 'opting out' proposal has generated nothing less than universal hostility from all sections of the educational establishment, including parent associations. There have also been serious reservations voiced by some Conservative MPs (*The Guardian*, 21 November 1987). The proposal is that the governing bodies of schools can apply to 'opt out' of local authority control and into central state control by becoming grant maintained schools. Such schools would then receive direct funding from the Department of Education and Science instead of the LEA, generating what Mrs Thatcher has called 'state independent schools'! Only a simple majority of school governors is required in order to be able to apply to the Secretary of State to become a grant maintained school. This decision must then be put to the parents of pupils attending the school at that time. Again, provided that a simple majority is achieved, and that the Secretary of State (who has the final say) is in agreement, the school will receive direct grant status. This Mrs Thatcher hopes will create a new system of education involving three types of school which would give a wider choice of public provision for those who are not satisfied with the current system.

Simon (1988) has noted that the main thrust of the Education Reform Bill is towards 'destabilizing locally controlled "systems" and, concomitantly, pushing the whole structure of schooling towards a degree, at least, of privatization, so establishing a base which could be further exploited later' (Simon, 1988:48). What Simon is hinting at here is the possibility of moving towards the introduction of educational vouchers and an 'independent education for all' (*The Independent*, 1 November 1988). The 'opting out' proposal as envisaged by Margaret Thatcher is not quite a voucher system but it is similar to it (Wilby and Midgley, 1987). Indeed, given the logic of Thatcherism, if schools do not 'opt out' in great numbers as envisaged by the Prime Minister, there will always be evidence of a few parents who perceive this to be an infringement of their individual freedom and consumer sovereignty. In such a situation, the introduction of a system of educational vouchers seems likely.

However, there is a complication when talking about educational vouchers because such a system has been advocated by those on the left as well as the right. The re-emerging interest in educational vouchers is often associated with Milton Friedman, although the original notion is attributed to Adam Smith in the late eighteenth century. The kind of educational voucher system which is being advocated by the right is one which approximates that favoured by Friedman – a straightforward system which gives every child the same 'pupil entitlement' (Hillgate Group, 1987:41). Goldberg has described this type of voucher scheme as the 'unregulated market model', in which all vouchers are of equal value and schools charge at the market rate (Snook, 1987; Le Grand and Robinson, 1984). Parents will therefore be left to pay any additional sum beyond the value of the voucher out of their new-found economic freedom provided by tax cuts.

There are two further aspects of the Education Reform Bill which I can do no more than briefly note (for a full discussion see Simon, 1988). First, the Government's intention to introduce the formal testing and assessment of pupils at the age of 7, 11, 14 and 16 also shows the influence of the radical right. This represents part of the attempt to provide parents with the necessary consumer information to decide which school to send their child to. Formal testing and the imposition of a 'core curriculum' is also seen as a way of increasing standards, because as Mrs Thatcher has asserted, even those schools which wish to stay under local authority control 'are going to have a core curriculum and they are going to have it because some schools have failed with children' (Thatcher, 1987). But as Simon has correctly stated, while the right want a *variety* of schools they also demand a 'strict *uniformity* in the curriculum where, they now claim, there is too much "variety"' (Simon, 1988:17). Therefore, despite the rhetoric of 'choice' and 'individual freedom', in practice the educational system is becoming *more* centrally controlled. The Education Reform Bill is estimated to give the Secretary of State for Education over 175 new powers. Clearly, the authoritarian concerns of the right take precedence over those of the 'free marketeers'.

Secondly, it is also worth drawing attention to the Government's attempt to tighten the bond between the products of schooling and the needs of industry. Following the introduction of the Technical and Vocational Education Initiative (TVEI) in 1983,[6] Kenneth Baker unveiled his reforming agenda for education with a pilot network of 20 centrally funded City Technology Colleges (CTCs) (*The Guardian*, 8 October 1987; DES, 1986). The intention of the CTCs, like TVEI, is to seek to develop the 'qualities of enterprise, self-reliance and responsibility, and secure the highest possible standards of achievement'. Despite the fact that these proposals were enthusiastically welcomed by Tory Party conference delegates, employers have been far less welcoming (Chitty, 1987). It has required a great deal of cajoling and additional government money to get the CTCs off the ground (*The Independent*, 24 February 1988). They also spell further chaos for local authorities who are trying to develop a rational response to the falling school population and improve the quality of local schools. I will say more about the 'new vocationalism', and the contradictions in the right's educational programme for reform in a moment, but first I want to note some of its strengths.

The right approach to educational domination

Twenty years ago the radical right were a small reactionary pressure group who were believed by many to have lost their place in the modern world. How they have come to dominate the educational debates of the 1980s would make a fascinating study. Those in the centre and on the left in British political and academic life have much to learn from their right-wing opponents about political lobbying, the manipulation of the media and forming political alliances, not to mention an ability to 'think the unthinkable'. It is also fair to say that the right have successfully hijacked the proper concerns which have been expressed by parents about the education of their children, particularly at a time of high youth unemployment. Yet it would be wrong to exaggerate the extent of the ideological battle which the right have had to fight in order to dominate the educational debate. The left offer little by way of a credible defence of comprehensive education, or a coherent set of policies which could improve the state of our schools (Lauder and Brown, 1988).

Moreover, despite the reactionary and backward-looking nature of new right policies for education they *appear* innovative and novel. The reason for this is noted by Phillips (1978:16):

> Twentieth Century Conservatives can no longer defend the status quo, for their principles no longer dominate any important Western society. Instead, they advocate reform – but reform in a vastly different direction from what either the liberals or radicals [on the left would] recommend.

A further strength of the right's populist appeal has been its focus on the failure of the Welfare State (including education) to gain the support of those whom it was intended to help. It is true to say that many working-class people do feel that the educational system is something which is imposed upon them, and is often irrelevant to their present and future lives, serving to do little more than attack their sense of dignity. Mrs Thatcher's (1987) appeal to 'involving people themselves, restoring their confidence in themselves, renewing their faith, reawakening their pride' is a powerful one. However, the policies offered by the right are seriously flawed and will lead to greater dependence and alienation.

From meritocracy to parentocracy

The educational system is standing on the verge of the 'third wave' in its sociohistorical development. The 'third wave' represents the rise of the *parentocracy*, where a child's education is dependent upon the wealth and wishes of parents, rather than the ability and efforts of pupils. To use the 'wave' analogy popularized by Toffler (1981), it can be argued that the 'first wave' involved the development of elementary state education for the 'lower orders'. The education of the working class was primarily concerned with the inculcation of basic information and knowledge seen to be appropriate for their predetermined (ascribed) place in society. This Dewey (1916) once described as the feudal dogma of social predestination.

The 'second wave' can be characterized as one involving a shift from an education determined by an accident of birth to one based upon 'age aptitude and ability'. Paramount importance is placed upon individual merit and achievement as a determinant of one's educational and occupational career. It must, however, be remembered that although the liberal democratic reforms since 1944 have been consistent with the ideology of meritocracy, and that important advances in educational performance of the working class have been achieved, they have not led to a significant improvement in life chances (Halsey *et al.*, 1980).

The third wave has been characterized in terms of the rise of the ideology of parentocracy. This involves a major programme of educational reform and privatization under the slogans of 'parental choice' and the 'free market'. The right have sought support for the third wave by suggesting that the policies they are advocating do not violate the spirit of the 1944 Education Act, because it clearly states that children should be educated in accordance with the wishes of their parents. However, this desperate attempt to legitimate the parentocracy is at best perfunctory. As Maclure (1968:223) has noted, in the 1944 Education Act:

> The parent's legal duty was changed from that of causing his [sic] child to receive 'efficient elementary instruction in reading, writing and arithmetic' to a duty to cause his child to receive 'efficient full-time education suitable to his age, aptitude and ability either by regular attendance at school or otherwise'.

Whereas the former was geared towards providing an appropriate education for the masses in terms of their social class and future destination in the social and occupational structure, the latter quite clearly states that one's education should be determined by age, aptitude and ability, not what parents, teachers or politicians think to be socially appropriate or expedient. We might ask, therefore, following the spirit of the Act, whether the best way of organizing the educational system for the 1990s is to let *parents* decide what the educational *potential* of their child is, and then let them judge what sort of school they should attend, if they can afford the fees?

This is not to deny that parents should be more involved in the running of our schools, and that choice of school should be as wide as possible. The most sensible strategy to adopt is one of getting parents involved in raising standards in *all* schools. The right's version of standards and choice seems to be somewhat different. When the right talk about standards they speak with a 'forked tongue' – what is good for us and what is appropriate for them. What is appropriate for them is the 3 R's and what is good for us is the privilege of an élite education to mould our future leaders for higher office.

Their conception of choice is based on the idea of consumer freedom, rather than trying to raise standards in all schools. Those schools that do not offer the product which parents want should lose their custom and go out of business. This is the consumer society gone mad. The idea that a private education is a better education because it has so far only been available to the wealthy does have some populist appeal. However, the reason why these schools exist is precisely in order to distinguish their 'product' from that of mass schooling. If everyone receives a voucher in order to buy an education, it will be the wealthy who have the ability to pay who will ensure that such educational and social distinctions are maintained, because this is precisely what they are paying for. What is on offer, therefore, is an absolute choice of *application* (i.e. you can apply where you want) but this does not mean an absolute choice of *school*. Some further selection will have to be made for the 'good' schools, which given the right's enthusiasm for an unregulated market form of educational voucher, is likely to be based upon an ability to pay. The notion of 'variety' and 'choice' in this context is therefore a sham. 'Variety' will mean failure for the vast majority because access to higher education and professional jobs depends upon the acquisition of academic qualifications.

Indeed, if we want to offer 'choice', it is not parents who should decide but the individual child. This is because parents have a tendency to raise and socialize their children in their own image, which may not meet the social or intellectual needs of the individual or society. In this context, selection and allocation will need to be delayed (this does not mean that pupil progress should not be monitored) as long as possible so that the individuals, in consultation with school counsellors, careers officers, teachers and parents, can make a considered judgement about their future educational needs. This is not only a more authentic notion of 'choice' in the educational context, but also recognizes that the extension of a fully comprehensive education holds the best chance of the educational system playing its part in meeting the social and economic challenge of the late twentieth century.

Towards a popular politics of education

A popular politics of education must resist the shift towards the parentocracy and its resulting inequalities. We should not attempt to hide from the fact that the educational system is in crisis, but show that its nature, causes and the policy responses which will be needed, are significantly different from those advanced by the right. The educational crisis in Britain is partly a result of cuts in educational expenditure and the deliberate attempt to destabilize and discredit the comprehensive school and the LEAs. However, there is a more deep-seated problem about what to teach to whom, because it is evident that a large proportion of young people from working-class backgrounds are not substantially benefiting from their time in secondary education. This problem has been intensified in many parts of Britain as a result of the collapse of job opportunities for school leavers in the early 1980s. The right's response has been to argue for different types of schools for different 'types' of children. Yet the growing tendency for pupils to question whether it is worth making an effort in school is premised on the fact that the overtly academic curriculum, and the hierarchical ordering of the school (so that only a few can make it no matter how hard pupils work), has alienated many of them from what should be a challenging and interesting period in their lives.

Although the shift to comprehensive schooling was of vital importance, it has not been the revolutionary change which the right have asserted. Private schools remain, and in some LEAs the tripartite system has not been disbanded. Vested social and educational interests have ensured that the grip of the academic curriculum has, if anything, been intensified as a result of comprehensive reorganization (Lowe, 1988). Therefore, a popular politics of education must question the wisdom of organizing our schools in a way which benefits a small minority at the expense of the majority of children. The learning of technical and practical knowledge and know-how remains a 'second-class' activity, suitable only for those who do not show an interest or the initiative to cope with an overly academic curriculum. A popular politics of education must be concerned with achieving a good standard of general education for all children, to empower them to confront the personal and social challenge of democratic citizenship in a way that allows them to go beyond the confines of their immediate experiences.

Another aspect of the educational crisis which needs to be addressed, concerns the severe restrictions on working-class educational and occupational advancement (Halsey *et al.*, 1980). The vested interests of the powerful and privileged have not only acted as a conservative force on the content and transmission of school knowledge, but have also restricted the opportunities for educational success and access to higher education to a predictably privileged few. I have argued elsewhere (Brown, 1987, 1988) that sociologists have commonly misunderstood the nature of working-class responses to school, yet it is evident that the limited opportunities for educational success have done little to generate a good general education for all pupils. Indeed, I know of no other advanced industrial society that has such restricted access to higher education, and been so successful in alienating their young people that, by the time they are 16 years old, many reject any kind of further education. A new deal for young people must, therefore, be built on the expansion of genuine opportunities for higher education, and must avoid the premature channelling of pupils into an educational cul-de-sac.

A popular politics of education must also challenge the economic wisdom of the parentocracy, which will have a profound impact on the selection and allocation of pupils for their future economic roles. We have seen that the parentocracy will make the educational system more and more an agency to train children to occupy the economic positions of their parents, despite the fact that many of the jobs their parents occupied have now disappeared (Blackman, 1987). Despite this there has been a much greater emphasis on vocational preparation in schools. The new vocationalism may be a way of ensuring that the working class do not get their hands on the real vocational prizes (Watts, 1983), or develop unrealistic occupational aspirations, but it will prove to be economically disastrous. This is because in an advanced, technologically based economy, it is essential that all have an equal chance of receiving the appropriate higher education and training so that the most able and hard working can be recruited for the most demanding jobs. Currently, we have skill shortages especially of technologists and engineers whose training requires a specialist education in polytechnics or universities. Yet it is precisely the *middle classes* who have dominated places in higher education who have *rejected* a career in industry (Brown, 1987).

If we are going to meet the economic as well as the social demands of an advanced capitalist democracy, we will require young women and men who are capable of responding to new opportunities, which will include periods of retraining but also allow them to benefit constructively from a shorter working week and a shorter working life. If Britain is to meet these demands we must resist the third wave and fight for a general education for all pupils during the compulsory school years.[7] In short, a popular politics of education must seek to break down class inequalities, and never lose sight of the fact that it must be built upon the principles of social justice, which must be dedicated to the pursuit of generating an educational system which goes as far as possible towards overcoming the *hereditary* curse of inequalities whether they are based upon class, gender or race.

In this chapter, I have attempted to show that the rise of the parentocracy is neither fair nor in the national interest. Its imposition is dominated by ideological rather than educational considerations, and will do little to meet the social, educational and economic challenges which now confront the educational system, however much the right have succeeded in laying claim to the real concerns which parents have about the education of their children. A popular politics of education must not shy away from such matters; neither need we be on the defensive. We must recognize the limitations of the comprehensive system as it has developed, and build upon the advances which have been made. There is no alternative to a comprehensive system of education because it offers the best foundation for overcoming the erosion of democracy and social justice which we are now witnessing, and of contributing to Britain's future economic prosperity.

Acknowledgements

I would like to thank Shane Blackman, Chris Harris, Hugh Lauder, Dick Scase and Richard Sparks for their comments on an earlier draft of this chapter.

Notes

1 The most outstanding example of this is that despite the Government's intention to abolish the Inner London Education Authority, no less than 94% of parents were against such a move (*The Independent*, 14 April 1988).
2 Compare this argument with that offered by the Centre for Contemporary Cultural Studies (1981).
3 No doubt Flew would see the New Right's grip on contemporary educational and social policy as a manifestation of *perestroika*.
4 This assertion is not supported by much of the available evidence, which suggests that the vast majority of teachers are far from politically motivated in the conduct of their professional duties (see Hargreaves, 1982; Lawn and Grace, 1987).
5 Shortage of space makes it impossible to discuss the Educational Reform Bill in any detail. There are, however, a number of good accounts of the Bill and its implications. The book by Simon (1988) is particularly informative (and inexpensive).
6 Moreover, TVEI was funded by the Manpower Services Commission rather than the DES.
7 After all, youth unemployment actually removes the need for vocational training at this stage because there will be ample time for 'training' once they reach school leaving age.

References

Baker, K. (1987). *The Guardian*, 8 October.
Bantock, G.H. (1977). An alternative curriculum. In *Black Paper 1977* (C.B. Cox and R. Boyson, eds). London: Temple Smith.
Belsey, A. (1986). The new right, social order and civil liberties. In *The Ideology of the New Right* (R. Levitas, ed.). Cambridge: Polity Press.
Blackman, S.J. (1987). The labour market in school: New vocationalism and issues of socially ascribed discrimination. In *Education, Unemployment and Labour Markets* (P. Brown and D.N. Ashton, eds). Lewes: Falmer Press.
Brown, P. (1987). *Schooling Ordinary Kids*. London: Tavistock.
Brown, P. (1988). Education and the working class: A cause for concern. In *Education: In Search of a Future* (H. Lauder and P. Brown, eds). Lewes: Falmer Press.
Centre for Contemporary Cultural Studies (1981). *Unpopular Education*. London: Hutchinson.
Chitty, C. (1987). City technology colleges. In *Aspects of Vocationalism* (C. Chitty, ed.). London: Institute of Education.

Cox, C.B. and Boyson, R. (eds) (1977). *Black Paper 1977*. London: Temple Smith.

Cox, C.B. and Dyson, A.E. (eds) (1968). *Fight for Education*. London: Critical Quarterly.

Department of Education and Science (1986). *City Technology Colleges: A New Choice of School*. London: DES.

Department of Education and Science (1987). *Statistical Bulletin* 2/87. London: DES.

Dewey, J. (1916). *Democracy and Education*. New York: Macmillan.

Flew, A. (1987). *Power to the Parents*. London: Sherwood Press.

Goldstein, H. and Cuttance, P. (in press). National assessment and school comparisons. *Journal of Educational Policy*.

The Guardian, 21 November 1987.

Halsey, A.H., Heath, A.F. and Ridge, J.M. (1980). *Origins and Destinations*. Oxford: Clarendon Press.

Hargreaves, D.H. (1982). *The Challenge for the Comprehensive School*. London: Routledge and Kegan Paul.

Hillgate Group (1986). *Whose Schools? A Radical Manifesto*. London: Claridge Press.

Hillgate Group (1987). *The Reform of British Education*. London: Claridge Press.

HMSO (1987). *Education Reform Bill*. London: HMSO.

Lauder, H. (1987). The new right and educational policy in New Zealand. *New Zealand Journal of Educational Studies*, **22**, 3–23.

Lauder, H. and Brown, P. (eds) (1988). *Education: In Search of a Future*. Lewes: Falmer Press.

Lawn, M. and Grace, G. (eds) (1987). *Teachers: The Culture and Politics of Work*. Lewes: Falmer Press.

Le Grand, J. and Robinson, R. (eds) (1984). *Privatisation and the Welfare State*. London: George Allen and Unwin.

Lowe, R. (1988). *Education in the Post-war Years: A Social History*. London: Routledge and Kegan Paul.

Maclure, J.S. (1968). *Educational Documents: England and Wales 1816–1968*. London: Methuen.

McPherson, A. and Willms, J.D. (1987). Equalisation and improvement. Some effects of comprehensive reorganisation in Scotland. *Sociology*, **21**(4), 509–540.

Phillips, N.R. (1978). *The Quest for Excellence*. New York: Philosophical Library.

Scruton, R. (1984). *The Meaning of Conservatism*. London: Macmillan.

Shor, I. (1986). *Culture Wars*. London: Routledge and Kegan Paul.

Simon, B. (1988). *Bending the Rules: The Baker 'Reform' of Education*. London: Lawrence and Wishart.

Snook, I. (1987). The voucher system: An alternative method of financing education. *New Zealand Journal of Educational Studies*, **22**, 25–34.

Thatcher, M. (1987). *The Independent*, 14 September.

Toffler, A. (1981). *The Third Wave*. London: Pan Books.

Watts, A.G. (1983). *Education, Unemployment and the Future of Work*. Milton Keynes: Open University Press.

Wilby, P. and Midgley, S. (1987). The future of schooling lies with the Tory radicals. *The Guardian*, 23 July.

Wright, N. (1983). Standards and the Black Papers. In *Education, Policy and Society* (B. Cosin and M. Hales, eds). London: Routledge and Kegan Paul.

Young, M. (1961). *The Rise of the Meritocracy*. Harmondsworth: Penguin.

4 Mass Communications

Richard Sparks and Ian Taylor

The enthusiasm of the inner-circles of the Thatcher Government for a radical reconstruction of British public broadcasting is quite unmistakable. The Thatcher Government was responsible, in March 1985, for commissioning the first-ever enquiry to query the continuing reliance of the British Broadcasting Corporation (BBC) on a revenue raised only by a combination of a public levy and a further subsidy by the State (HMSO, 1986), and it was also responsible for encouraging the chairman of that enquiry, Professor Alan Peacock, whom it believed would support the radical revision of the financial relations between the BBC and the State, to report quickly and without unnecessary delay. No matter that this particular initiative seems now to have encountered some obstacles, reports from and about the series of private seminars on the future of broadcasting held at Downing Street in September 1987[1] suggest that new policy proposals to weaken the hegemonic position which the BBC currently enjoys over broadcasting in Britain, particularly in economic (and therefore in institutional) respects, are unlikely to be postponed for long.

In part, the problem which the Government (and indeed many other observers) are identifying here is straightforwardly fiscal, and concerns the size of the subsidy which the BBC requires from the State. The informed consensus is that the growth of advertising revenue for the commercial television companies, which is likely to escalate even further over the coming decade, will ensure, unless additional appropriations are forthcoming from the public purse, that the BBC will inevitably encounter what is referred to as a revenue crisis.

The pressure for change in the current form of organization of British broadcasting undoubtedly also arises, in part from a generalized imperative born of the proliferation of new mass media technologies (the growth of videotape, the development of multichannel satellite television and cable, and a range of other developments in the computer field). It is no part of our argument here to deny the existence, popularity or dynamic potential of these developments, but it is very much our argument that the emergence of the new media technology in no way constitutes an argument for the abandonment of the idea of a public television broadcasting system.

There is no doubt that the current attack on the BBC (and, thereby, by implication, on any idea of an institutionalized and State-supported system of public broadcasting) derives, in particular, from a partisan, political belief which is deeply held among many of the most currently influential sectors of the Conservative Party – namely, that the BBC is irretrievably biassed, in some fundamental sense (deriving from the BBC's own institutional history and structure), against the kind of radical change which this Government has initiated and carried through in Britain over the last 10 years. In this particular respect, of course, the critiques of the BBC that have been forthcoming from radical right political circles very closely reflect many of the critiques which have been mounted of that same institution by some scholars on the left: namely, that the BBC is an unaccountable and simultaneously a hierarchical and bureaucratic apparatus, operating (especially, but not exclusively, at moments of crisis) faithfully within an extraordinarily narrow high bourgeois/aristocratic conception of the national interest. For right-wing critiques, of course, the problem that this reality presents is not that it excludes or marginalizes from serious (or 'authorized') public debate the views of the socialist opposition and organized labour, of feminism and anti-sexist constituencies, the peace movement, or anti-racist groups and discourses. It is, rather, that the continuing domination of British broadcasting by a certain, familiar comforting voice of authority tends to problematize the right's project of radical-populism, concerned as this is to create and disperse a vigorous new commonsense conception of self-reliance and individualism throughout civil society.

We shall return to the ostensibly political critique of the BBC as a national institution a little later. In the meantime, we do need to see, however, that these more straightforwardly fiscal and political critiques of the existing form of public-sector broadcasting in Britain are also underlined and given a conclusive elaboration in conservative circles – and in many other key arenas – by a broader and essentially philosophical argument. In its most general terms, drawn without qualification from the work of Friedrich von Hayek, this argument is one part of the headlong attack on 'statism' to which this Government is theologically committed: *all* concentrations of State power and authority other than the law itself (which is the necessary guarantor of predictability and trust in the free market economy), *are* (in this perspective) seen as unwarrantable and dangerous monopolies, threatening the liberty of individuals and the market itself. Enthusiasts for free-market solutions to the broadcasting problem in and around the Thatcher Government are also clearly convinced that the BBC (and the associated duopolistic 'system' that has dominated British broadcasting since the 1950s) has an unwarrantably advantaged position in the television and broadcasting marketplace, and that all kinds of economic and cultural advantages would flow from a break-up of the existing system. It is not only, in this view, that the broadcasting system (and especially television) represents what the Prime Minister herself calls the 'last bastion of trade union restrictive practice', it is also that there is no good philosophical rationale for the continued existence of the BBC, as currently organized, as an exceptional institution, untouched by the broader revolution that is sweeping the British economy and the civil society generally, as a result of the 'freeing of the market forces'.[2]

We think it is important to recognize, however, that the thrust of this philosophical critique of the 'statist' public-sector broadcasting as an inert, reactionary form is now being vigorously and effectively pursued not only by spokespeople of the Thatcher Government, but also by informed, articulate professionals within the broadcasting industry. It is easy to dismiss some of the support that is being given to the radical revision of public broadcasting and to the introduction of free-market principles as being a more or less unambiguous reflection of economic self-interest on the part of journalists who happen to be well-placed to profit from impending changes. It is certainly very difficult to separate the fashionably clever critique of public-sector broadcasting advanced by Peter Jay (articulated entirely around the 'level of access' - or choice - which this system affords the viewer) from the reality of Mr Jay's role in the foundation of the ill-starred TV-AM and the interest he continues to hold in a variety of other, potentially rather more profitable, companies. By the same token, of course, any commentary which might be made by Mr Rupert Murdoch on these issues would have to be understood in terms of the controlling interest he owns in *Sky Television*, an international company working on the simultaneous broadcasting of programmes across Europe by satellite.

But there *is* now widespread public evidence of a loss of faith on the part of many working journalists and even by system managers in the viability and dynamic potential of public-sector broadcasting,[3] and there are also many very creative and progressive-minded journalists who seem persuaded by some version of free market philosophy as applied to the radical reconstruction of broadcasting. So, for example, according to David Graham, a major independent producer of good television programmes and a member of the so-called *Twenty-five Per Cent group*,[4] the fundamental weaknesses of the existing ('regulated') system are that it is stagnating, inefficient and far too narrow. Unlike Peter Jay, who is on record as believing that *the* most important criterion for the evaluation of broadcasting is the question of 'accessibility' to the broad mass of the audience (the 'consumers'), Graham, as an independent producer, claims to be concerned with the quality of programming and, in particular, with encouraging creativity on the part of broadcasting professionals. He believes that television in Britain takes too few risks and that, in particular, television journalists operate within a very narrow, restricted range of understandings as to the interests of their audience. For him, this essentially 'habitual' and familiar set of journalistic practices is a function of the relative absence of competition in British television (and, in particular, the continuing presence of only four channels, each with its own relatively predictable and undisturbed mandate and audience). He points admiringly, by comparison, to the remarkable improvement in comedy shows that has occurred on American prime-time television (*Cheers, The Cosby Show, Taxi, Night Court*, etc.) which he sees to be a function of the increasingly vigorous competitive environment which ABC-, CBS- and NBC-affiliated stations encounter in each local television market within the United States. And so, finally, he does believe that there is no necessary contradiction (as he accuses too many liberal and social democratic commentators of believing) between, on the one hand, the idea of endowing consumers with the freedom to choose between a mass of competing television products and, on the other, the resultant quality of programming.[5] For David Graham, as an independent producer, the priorities of the upcoming revision of broadcasting legislation and policy ought, indeed, to be firmly orientated to the interests of viewers as choice-making consumers; and to the weakening of the overall power and influence of the BBC and, indeed, of the increasingly inert 'alliance' of the BBC and the Independent Broadcasting Authority (IBA), whose duopolistic domination of television now clearly obstructs innovation and experimentation in television.

Given all that is written and known about the conservative and hierarchical character of the BBC, in particular, over the last 60 years, it is not altogether surprising that the application of radical free market ideas to broadcasting should now be attracting support among bright and creative journalists. That it should be doing so should alert socialist and other progressive critics to the dangers involved in assuming that the visionary and strategic thinking of the Government on broadcasting will encounter a uniform opposition from within the BBC or the BBC/IBA 'complex' as a whole. It is certainly going to be unhelpful, we would argue, for progressive critics to respond to new market initiatives simply by insisting (by analogy, say, to the newspaper industry) on the *inevitable* inability of a free-market system to deliver a set of differentiated, pluralistic products;[6] and we are also unpersuaded by the pleas of *ad hoc* organizations like the Broadcasting Research Unit, for the recognition and preservation of the 'delicate balance' that is involved in the existing BBC-IBA duopoly.[7] We doubt, in particular, whether arguments of this kind have a real purchase with the more thoughtful and creative professional broadcasters who have experienced the timidity and traditionalism that has characterized this 'delicate balance', especially in recent years.

We are also very conscious in this respect, that one of the many consequences of the transformations of 'Thatcherism', with respect both to dominant political and to popular commonsense, is the increasing identifications of the idea of *the nation*, or more particularly of the national interest, with the idea of *the Market* and the idea of a dynamic so-called 'Enterprise Culture'. In such a context, the appeals that are made by organizations like the Broadcasting Research Unit to the idea of broadcasting performing a 'public service' in the interests of the nation as a whole – conceived of as *a community* – may be interpreted, certainly in many Conservative circles, as an essentially reactionary deceit which they oppose to the new realities of the social market economy.

The problem confronting progressive defenders of the idea of public broadcasting is akin to the general problem that currently confronts defenders of the ideas of public provision, public service and the public sphere as a whole in Thatcher's Britain. There is a pressing need to be able to formulate the opposition to free market initiatives in and through a perspective which does not collapse into a defence of the unhappy and unpopular reality of the bureaucratic Welfare State or, indeed, to the defence of existing structures of authority and privilege (including, indeed, the privileged position that has been enjoyed by the liberal middle class – Peter Jay's 'educated classes' – within the Keynesian Welfare State and its associated career systems). There is a need to find a perspective that is less compromised than that of Keynesian Welfare State liberalism and a need, also, to find a distinctive new language in which to formulate an oppositional, or alternative, perspective with any chance of having a broad popular influence;[8] equally, with any hope of disconnecting significant sections of Conservative or Liberal/Democratic opinion from the ideological couplet that fuses the idea of nation with the overwhelming, uncritical embrace of free-market theory and its denunciation of 'the state'.

We are arguing, in fact, that the rhetoric of 'freedom' in 'free market' theory has the effect of incorporating the liberal within the Thatcherite coalition (and that nowhere is this more apparent than among articulate and creative communications and media professionals).[9] The fatalistic presumption that consumer goods define the 'public good' is difficult to resist when it is presented as a given premise that the explosion of channels and media constitutes a liberation from the anachronistic, corporate stasis of the broadcasting duopoly. The displacement of broadcasting by the new technologies is thus presented in terms of a narrative emphasizing modernization, which only the nostalgic and undemocratic will resist: futile resistance at that.

But we want to argue that it is not inevitable that all resistance to this process has to fall into the trap of what McLuhan has called 'rear-view mirrorism' (the tendency to evaluate a new medium in terms derived from the one it has displaced). An historical parallel is particularly instructive here. The current arguments are curiously and closely analogous to those conducted between John Ruskin and John Stuart Mill in an earlier era of rapid social and technological development, in the early 1860s, though they rarely achieve the same passion or precision.

We do not refer to this as a mere (historical) curiosity. The familiarity of the argument reminds us that the 'modernizing' posture of Thatcherism is historically continuous with classical liberalism. It is an old argument in a new manifestation – and much of Ruskin's existing rebuttal remains valid for it.

Ruskin developed his own, resolutely Christian, social theory in a dialogue of opposition with 'political economy' as it occurred in the work of Ricardo, Smith and Mill, as well as innumerable lesser lights. Ruskin also knew that he wrote against the current of the times, and in a situation where the political economists wrote as torch-bearers of 'progress', and it is perhaps for this reason that Ruskin allowed himself to be styled old-fashioned. Thus he declared himself 'a violent Tory of the old school' (Ruskin, 1985:23). There is an element of teasing in this. But Ruskin was, clearly, quite acutely aware that in an era when the orthodoxy had a bland confidence in progress, the dissidence of revolutionaries and reactionaries can look uncomfortably alike (an awkwardness which was, perhaps, also experienced by Adorno in our own century).

The essence of Ruskin's objection to the political economists is that they have no adequate concept of society, except as an aggregation of contracting and exchanging individuals. This is both an analytic and an ethical complaint. Analytically, Ruskin holds that individualism of the Millian variety is an insufficient basis for a theory of economic life; still less adequate for a general theory of social action (even if, that is, economic exchange is taken to be paradigmatic of social action generally). Ruskin's view is that political economy is based on a theory of human nature, in which calculation is primary and 'social affections' merely accidental; for him, this is so far mistaken as to render all the conclusions arrived at by the political economists uninteresting, except by virtue of their malign practical consequences. Thus, the politico-economic view is 'democratic' only in so far as it reduces *all* social actors to the status of 'engines'. This reduction, Ruskin argues, makes it impossible for the political economist to distinguish between 'the greatest average of work' obtained and 'the real amount... of good rendered'. Thus, what may be called the consequentialist morality of political economy is self-defeating because, centred on the calculation of expediency, it provides no means either for knowing or evaluating the outcome of the transaction. This is destructive, in Ruskin's view, in that it generates no account of social obligation or association. It depends on the extension of an economic metaphor, inadequate even in that sphere, to areas of life where it has no applicability (Ruskin, 1985:167).

There is a direct connection here between Ruskin's economic writings and his aesthetic views, particularly when he turns his attention to the concept of value. Ruskin alights gleefully on Mill's definition of wealth as the possession of a 'large stock of useful articles' (Ruskin, 1985:209) and turns it against him. Such a definition depends, Ruskin argues, on a prior specification of utility: if wealth requires both possession and use, then the growth of wealth depends on the development of a 'correlative human capacity' to use. This revision, which makes the notion of wealth dependent in Ruskin's terms, not merely on a 'have' but also on a 'can', introduces a contingency which actually subverts Mill's intention because:

> Three-fourths of the demands existing in the world are romantic; founded on visions, idealisms, hopes and affections; and the regulation of the purse is, in its essence, regulation of the imagination and the heart. Hence, the right discussion of the nature of price is a very high metaphysical and psychical problem (Ruskin, 1985:215).

This being so, Ruskin wants to argue, there can be no clear separation between areas regulated entirely by markets and those where moral and aesthetic consideration obtain. This necessarily has a paradoxical consequence. On the one hand, the simple fact that 'demands' exceed any plodding and material definition of 'utility' subverts the political economist's attempted calculation. On the other hand, however, the market tends to constrain the nature of those demands which can be either articulated or met.

These arguments have clear contemporary echoes. The modern inheritors of political economy know perfectly well that the contemporary broadcasting and other cultural industries constitute a market for 'goods' whose 'utility' is not straightforwardly calculable. That is to say, in every case in advertising as much as entertainment, the awareness of 'visions, idealisms, hopes and affections' is intrinsic to the marketability of cultural goods. But Ruskin anticipates the modern exponents of the free market in culture and their frequently voiced argument that whatever sells is what is wanted. [10] What is absolutely pivotal for Ruskin, is the uneasy and frequently unsatisfactory relationship between what is produced for sale or consumption and the continuing and pressing demands of 'consumers' for the satisfaction of their dreams and ideas. Certainly, one cannot have it both ways: it is not reasonable to argue both that the market is about 'visions, idealisms, hopes and affections' and yet that it is immune to aesthetic, moral and political considerations.

Ruskin's aesthetic theory is closely attentive to the public place and function of aesthetic forms: hence his lifelong concern with architecture. Thus, for example, the beauty of the Gothic cathedral is only *intelligible* as the public monument of the society which built it, only *conceivable* in relation to a whole network of social powers and institutions and only *practically achievable* under less alienated conditions of labour than those which obtain in industrial production.

In this particular sense, artistic creation and social regulation are not in stark opposition, which is how they are seen in neoliberal market theory; rather they are in a dynamic relation of constraint and empowerment. Architecture has a massive physical and social presence which may sometimes oppress and alienate those who have to live with it, but it can also express and echo the local culture or the general aspirations of a people; and it can sometimes do all of these things simultaneously.

We do think that these understandings have a direct relevance for the contemporary debate around public broadcasting and television. It is, after all, illogical for a Government committed to free market theory to be invoking a notion of a 'moral standard' (as it has done with increasing frequency since 1984) in respect to cinema, videotape and television, or indeed, to be referencing some notion of 'fairness' or bias in television (as spokespeople like Norman Tebbit have done, repetitively, with respect to news and current affairs programming) without also recognizing that such notions must have a definite social basis – that they do invoke, indeed, some notion of a *public sphere*, or set of *social relations*, or (perish the thought) *community value* that is independent of the free play of market forces.

A democratic and realistic conclusion

In part, our argument here is simply that the free market theorists have no understanding of, and perhaps no interest in, history and culture. The preoccupation of recent converts to free market theory with a discourse of modernism and of entrepreneurial creativity suppresses and/or ignores some stubborn empirical realities. So, for example, the truth is that the BBC, for all that its current affairs and news programming appears to be irresistibly couched, especially in forms of language and presentation, in a comfortable but extraordinarily restricted world view, retains a very significant viewing audience and a broad allegiance across the whole of society.[11] It does this, we would suggest, by virtue of its continuing ability to attract and retain a very significant number of talented journalists, presenters, writers of drama and of comedy, sportspeople and entertainers, for whom the BBC, for all its limitations, remains the primary route into public consciousness and debate within Britain and for whom, indeed, the continuing existence of such a sphere of *national public debate* (or of a national 'stage' on which to *entertain* or to *perform* – as in sport) is an important value (and certainly just as important as the level of fees which they receive). There is surely an important sense in which the existence of such a public sphere is both the precondition for, and the most serious available challenge to, an artist, entertainer or politician who is genuinely interested in the public acceptance of his or her talents, professional abilities, or political projects and platforms. One has only to look at societies like the United States and Canada in order to see what the absence of any such accepted national 'stage' does to the standard and character (*and* the real public appeal and popularity) of prime-time television. There is no necessary contradiction in new, dynamic commercial channels forming *part* of the public sphere; but we do say that such new channels *must* connect with, and give voice to, the great variety of regional, class and ethnic cultures which compose the complex social formation that is 'Britain'.

A key element in our argument is that the free market theorists who are at work in the reform of public sector broadcasting may seriously underestimate not only the cultural and historical importance, but also the continuing popularity, of the kind of television with which the BBC has historically been associated. The two BBC channels continue to attract some 48% of the television audience; thereby posing a serious challenge to the view that ITV is *the* channel for 'the masses'. More particularly, the BBC has consistently performed well in its ability to give expression to important areas of popular interest (comedy, sport, leisure, morning television and drama).

We do not advance these arguments in the belief that they will have any immediate influence over the impending, radical reform of British broadcasting policy. But, for reasons to which we have already alluded, we do take it that there will continue to be immense interest among the citizenry of Britain in the precise form and content of the television system that will replace the existing BBC/ITV duopoly. We want to enrol as large a section of opinion as possible in the defence of the notion of the public sphere in broadcasting, even in a deregulated market consisting of several new channels, in which the BBC will be at a substantial economic disadvantage. Our key 'philosophical', not to say cultural and sociological, observation is that free market theorists fundamentally downplay the importance of *national*, *public* television as a popular-cultural terrain in Britain.

We take it more or less as given, therefore, that any significant shift in the form and content of television in the direction, simply, of entertainment (in the manner of recent American experience) will meet considerable resentment and resistance at many levels of British society. It will be vital to marshal these anxieties and the implicit national consensus around quality, pluralism and social relevance which, we argue, remains a widespread, popular expectation in Britain, in the form of a specific policy agenda.

We can sketch out here some elements of what that agenda might include. We suggest, for instance, that while there may indeed be persuasive reasons (articulated by David Graham and others) for the inclusion of market initiatives in the *production* of television programmes, such arguments are far less compelling (or indeed clear) in respect of the evaluation of such programmes at the point of their reception. We consider that there is still strong support for some kind of corporatist regulation of television, in which relevant bodies take careful responsibility for assessing the programming which television professionals produce. However, any such body must be far less centralized and bureaucratically dominated than currently proposed. Councils should correspond geographically to the regions covered by television companies. They should be composed, we propose, of some elected members of local authorities as well as some circulating representation from local interest groups. We envisage such local television councils as being in the nature of consumer councils, but they should proceed in recognition of the fact that the television audience is composed of a broad range of citizens, holding widely differing, legitimate social and cultural interests. It is important, too, that such councils should be able to conceive of the activity of 'viewing' as more than the passive consumption of a market product. For this reason, civil servants and agents of the television companies themselves should have only minority representation on television councils at the local level. It should be part of the responsibility of local television councils to adjudicate in concrete and specific terms on the performance of television companies operating in their locality, and to extend this evaluation to an assessment of the companies' ability to reflect and give voice to forms of cultural practice and interest important within the regional population, as well as to issues of local or national political importance.

We take it that these regional television councils ought to report simultaneously and directly to a National Television Council, with some significant representation at that level of programme producers and television professionals. But we do not accept that the mandate and responsibility of any such National Council could replace that of Parliament itself, which ought to have the direct and unchallenged responsibility for assessing, on a regular basis, the performance by television companies of their public tasks. The regular reports produced by regional television councils ought to be of considerable help and importance in the adjudications of Parliament, while the commentaries provided by the National Television Council, which ought always to be public documents given full airing and discussion in the public access and current affairs programmes of each local station, ought also to be important instruments in the evaluation of the performance by each regional station, set against a national standard, but actually applied, none the less, in recognition of differences of public 'interest' in each locality.

We are trying here, in part, to think through a problem on which many other students of broadcasting policy have commented – namely, the problem of how to give teeth to the existing legislation of Parliament on the performance of television and, in particular, how to give life to that legislation in the process of examining and awarding licences to television companies. It is apparent that the existing licensing procedures do not always firmly ensure the adherence of companies to standards of representation demanded by Parliament. It is also apparent that the assessment of the performance of the existing BBC programming, both at the national and local levels, is carried out extremely unsatisfactorily by the BBC's Board of Governors; a Board that appears to be responsible to 'the State' only at moments of crisis as defined by the Government, and representative as it is only of a very narrow, and rather well-worn, range of political and cultural opinion in Britain. That is, the Board of the BBC appears *only* to be responsible to the Government at the precise moment when it ought least to be so: that is, over the broadcasting of *particular* politically controversial programmes, e.g. the *Real Lives* controversy.

In making proposals for the creation of an entirely new set of institutions for overseeing and assessing the operation of already existing television companies, as well as of companies that are about to be created, and also of the BBC in whatever form it is retained, we are trying to think through the problem of representing the notion of a public sphere as it is discussed, in particular, in the work of John Ruskin and in his nineteenth-century critique of political economy. We are also trying to follow through our own injunction, i.e. to connect to the commonsense assumptions and understandings which people in Britain bring to their everyday watching of television. These everyday uses of television are quite variable, but they are the result of traditions and practices endemic to social relations and to this particular cultural formation: they are not simply the effects of the whim of producers or viewers. Television systems *can* be integral to the defence and development of the public sphere – to the activity of what Raymond Williams called 'talking together about the processes of our common life'. But they can also serve as both a testament and a vehicle of its abandonment.

Notes

1 According to *The Times* (22 September 1987), participants in this meeting were left in no doubt that 'television is to be substantially expanded, with a larger number of channels, as in the United States, and funded by advertising or viewer subscription'.

2 Informed opinion at the end of 1987 anticipated the publication of a White Paper during 1988, and the introduction of 'a wide-ranging broadcasting Bill which should reach the statute book by the summer of 1989' (*The Times*, 22 September 1987).

3 For one such rather morose and deterministic analysis of the BBC as 'suffering from the sclerosis that tends eventually to affect all institutions and organisations', see Morgan (1986). Another example of the defeatist kind of analysis that pervades the world of professional managers in the broadcasting industry is the resigned set of observations recently advanced by John Howkins, the executive director of the International Institute of Communications, on the demise of the very idea of a broadcasting policy and its replacement instead by 'industrial policy' (Howkins, 1988).

4 These remarks of David Graham as to the potentialities of 'deregulation' in broadcasting were given in the course of the session on the Media at the Fabian Society's conference on *Beating the Blues*, held at the Polytechnic of the South Bank, London 4–5 December 1987.

5 This seems a rather optimistic interpretation. It is also true that exactly the same commercial dynamic which pours effort and resources into prime-time (which is prepared to spend $1 million per episode on *Miami Vice*) is responsible for packing the outer reaches of the schedule with endless repeats, cheap old films, quizzes and chat shows. Moreover, the character of television output is determined as much by international as by local markets: big commercial television budgets are only forthcoming if the product is serially marketable in other countries. The notion that independent quality television producers would benefit most, and gain most access to network broadcasting in a deregulated market (or, more particularly, that overall seriousness or creativity throughout the schedule would improve) is not convincing. The tendency will be towards a certain cosmopolitanism, wherein *Dallas* is available everywhere, while programmes which do not 'travel' particularly well but which may have an intense local and even national interest are likely to have to struggle.

6 This seems to be an underlying assertion, for example, in a recent analysis of the prospects for broadcasting in Britain presented by John Ellis. He argues that:

> In its next phase broadcasting...seems likely to be constituted by the haphazard results of large-scale gambles by media entrepreneurs. There will be precious little of 'the freedom' promised to producers or consumers. The level of financial risk is too great (Ellis, 1986:7).

7 Cf. Broadcasting Research Unit (1986). This pamphlet takes the form of a list and a discussion of eight principles which need to be 'retained within whatever systems are devised to provide broadcasting as new communications technologies come into use'. Without the recognition of these principles in any future broadcasting system, the BRU believes, begging rather a lot of issues, 'we shall be diminished as a nation'.

8 This emphasis on the need for a new 'language of opposition' in Britain is very much a feature of the recent writing of Sheila Rowbotham (1988), which exhibits a similar interest to our own, in the retrieval of the ideas of Ruskin, Morris and Carpenter.

9 Our reference here to 'a Thatcherite coalition' is not intended to imply the existence of a thoroughgoing agreement between liberal professionals working in the media and the Government *at the level of political or cultural preferences*. There is clearly a great tension between the economic neoliberalism of this Government and its keen embrace, since 1984, of censorious legislative control of the media (which is now exhibited in the creation of the Broadcasting Standards Council). The telling point, from our perspective, is how the Government's adherence to the idea of a 'minimal state', external to production, allows Government spokespeople to advance more than one argument at once. Hence 'Thatcherism' is not greatly discomfited by the fact of its fiscal policy or its cultural politics having an *uneven* appeal to different political interests and constituencies: Thatcherism straddles the potential antagonism of morally agnostic neoliberals and moral conservatives by providing them with a common adversary in the form of the corporatist power of the BBC and IBA. It offers neoliberals the prospect that the BBC/IBA 'duopoly' can be prised apart by market forms. Meanwhile, it reassures moral conservatives, in whose name Mrs Mary Whitehouse claims to speak, that the resulting disposition of forces will be more accountable to pressure from viewer-lobbyists and more easily made subject to legislative control. The reconciliation between these apparently competing positions, therefore, is found in the argument that the control of content should be removed from internal self-censorship by codes of practice and replaced by external oversight by legislation.

10 Ruskin remarks tersely: 'I use the word "demand" in a somewhat different sense from economists usually. They mean by it "the quantity of a thing sold"....In good English a person's "demand" signifies, not what he gets, but what he asks for' (Ruskin, 1985:208). Ruskin demands definitions from the political economists, and much of *Unto This Last* consists in his examination of their notions of 'value', 'wealth' and 'usefulness'. His harshest censure is reserved for Ricardo's 'usual inaccuracy' in his definition of the 'natural rate of wages'. Ironically it is Ruskin (whose economics are fundamentally derived from natural law) who takes the 'science of political economy' to task for its inadequate empirical basis and inaccurate social observation. He regards it as

a formalism – invalidated by its disconnection of economics from culture and value.

11 In 1987, for example, the audience 'take-up' of BBC 1 and BBC 2 was 12 hours and 28 minutes per week per head of population (as against only 10 hours and 28 minutes in 1982): ITV and Channel 4 recorded an average 12 hours and 56 minutes in 1987 as against 10 hours and 20 minutes in 1982 (the year before the introduction of Channel 4) (BARB/AGB 1987, figures supplied by BBC Audience Research). The BBC's share of the viewing audience does tend to vary slightly across social class lines, but in 1985 it still 'captured' some 44% of the total viewing of social class groups C2 and DE; as against some 56% of the AB category (Lamaison and Moreton, 1985). Perhaps even more interesting for our argument here is the very high level of satisfaction which the audience exhibits, in opinion surveys, with respect to the quality of BBC television programming: on a 'Quality of Output Index' devised by BBC Audience Research, the BBC scored 73/100 among viewers for the quality of its programmes, as against 69/100 for ITV. It is extremely significant for our argument here that the BBC's lead over ITV is greatest in what the Audience Research Department calls 'non-news or current affairs serious programmes' (see Samuels, 1985). On these and related issues, the rather more extensive and detailed examination of the viewing and listening audience provided by Morrison (1987) suggests that there is a very widespread interest and concern among the citizens as to the quality and variety of TV and radio programming alike.

References

Broadcasting Research Unit (1986). *The Public Service Idea in British Broadcasting – Main Principles*. London: Broadcasting Research Unit.

Ellis, J. (1986). Broadcasting and the State: The experience of Channel 4. *Screen*, **27** (3/4), 7.

HMSO (1986). *Report on the Committee on Financing the BBC*. Cmnd 9824. London: HMSO.

Howkins, J. (1988). Split screen. *The Listener*, 14 April, pp. 15–16.

Lamaison, J. and Moreton, J. (1985). Trends in viewing and listening 1985. *Annual Review of BBC Broadcasting Research Findings*, **12**, 11.

Morgan, J. (1986). The BBC and the concept of public service broadcasting. In *The BBC and Public Sector Broadcasting* (C. MacCabe and O. Stewart, eds). Manchester: Manchester University Press.

Morrison, D. (1987). *Invisible Citizens: British Public Opinion and the Future of Broadcasting*. London: John Libby.

Rowbotham, S. (1988). An inhuman society. *New Society*, April, p. 23.

Ruskin, J. (1985). *Unto this Last and Other Writings* (edited by Clive Wilmer). Harmondsworth: Penguin.

Samuels, J. (1985). The public's attitude to the funding of the BBC. *Annual Review of BBC Broadcasting Research Findings*, **12**, 46.

5 Race and Racism

Mark Mitchell and Dave Russell

Introduction

It is now widely accepted that the issue of race has shifted in recent years
from the periphery to the centre of British politics. Some writers go so far
as to argue that race is a key organizing principle within the ideology of
Thatcherism, a 'leading issue' that has shaped and directed the
progressive 'racialization' of politics in Britain in the 1970s and 1980s
(Centre for Contemporary Cultural Studies, 1982). In general, it has
become something of a commonplace to assert that the last two decades
have witnessed the emergence of a distinctive form of New Right racist
discourse in Britain.

Our task in this chapter is threefold. First, we shall question the
assumption that there is a cosy ideological 'fit' between this new racism
and the political credo of the New Right, particularly since New Right
ideology is itself an unstable amalgam of contradictory ideas. Secondly,
we shall examine the extent to which this new racism has been translated
into concrete policies by successive Thatcher governments or whether,
as with other strands of Thatcherism, there exists in the sphere of race a
considerable gap between New Right political rhetoric and the reality of
New Right policy and practice. Thirdly, we shall suggest that the relative
failure of anti-racist initiatives, in particular those developed by some
Labour-controlled local authorities, can only in part be blamed on the
New Right. We believe that the assumptions and principles underlying
many of these anti-racist initiatives are fundamentally misguided and
that the authoritarian way in which they have often been implemented
has alienated sections of the community, both black and white, whose

support is crucial if such initiatives are to succeed. Thus the failure to secure a wider legitimacy for anti-racism cannot be laid entirely at the door of the New Right. Any attempt to move beyond Thatcherism in the sphere of race policy and practice will have to come not only from a critique of the New Right, but also from a fundamental re-examination of the strategy and tactics of sections of the new urban left.

New Right? New racism?

In the last 20 years, it has been the social authoritarian rather than the market liberal wing of the New Right that has dominated policy debates about race. In general, neoliberal thinking has been absent from the rag-bag of traditional conservative and xenophobic nationalist ideas that are said to constitute a 'new racism' (Barker, 1981; Gordon and Klug, 1986). Although more prominent in the United States, neoliberal analyses of race and ethnicity in Britain have been confined to a few relatively obscure contributions.[1] Furthermore, these 'free market' ideas coexist uneasily with the race thinking that has been popularized in recent years by the social authoritarians.[2]

The most obvious area of agreement between the two competing New Right perspectives lies in their mutual hostility towards attempts by the State to outlaw racial discrimination and eliminate racial disadvantage. However, a different logic lies behind this common front against 'the race relations industry'. Neoconservative new racism generally resorts, in coded terms, to instinctivist theories to explain why such State intervention cannot work. Neoliberals add to this theme by suggesting that any attempt to outlaw racial discrimination through the use of coercive legislation, or indeed any form of anti-racist State intervention, will only cause further racial friction and thus worsen race relations (Davies, 1985; Daljord, 1985:218). However, it is important to note that their neoliberal convictions make some writers hostile, not only to race relations legislation and other forms of State intervention against discrimination, but also to the immigration laws (Davies, 1985). So, while Enoch Powell and the new race conservatives focus in a mystical way on the need to preserve the cultural identity of the British nation, 'extreme' neoliberalism denounces the very idea of treating individuals differently according to the group to which they belong.

Some neoliberals share with the new Powellite racism the view that it is indeed a basic truth that 'like prefers to be with like' and that people should always have the right to choose freely which cultural groups they wish to identify and associate with (Daljord, 1985:218). However, neoliberals tend to reject the idea that the cultural characteristics of ethnic groups are immutable since, given the opportunity and incentive, groups are capable of adapting their behaviour and attitudes. This kind of argument has been advanced most notably by black American social scientists (Sowell, 1983; Williams, 1982) who both maintain that market processes are the most effective means of removing irrational discrimination and enabling disadvantaged ethnic groups to climb the economic ladder of success (Majewski, 1988).

On closer examination there appear to be at least three major differences between the social authoritarian and market liberal analyses of race. First, there is a major tension between the neoconservative belief in a transcendent and exclusive form of British nationhood and the commitment of neoliberalism to individual liberty irrespective of racial identity. Thus, while the law and order rhetoric of conservative nationalism has looked to 'strong state' remedies to deal with the problems presented by a riotous and disorderly black population, libertarian arguments have warned against mobilizing the coercive power of the State against racial minorities in an over-oppressive manner (Ashford, 1985:33–4). Secondly, there is a world of difference between the alacrity with which the social authoritarians wish to impose the brutal choice of either 'repatriation' or 'compulsory incorporation' on minority black groups, and the anxiety of neoliberals to expand choice and freedom within a socially and culturally diverse society. Such an ideological opposition has been particularly evident in recent controversies about the education of black children, where outright rejection by the social authoritarians of multicultural education in favour of assimilationist schooling contrasts strongly with a neoliberal advocacy of the education voucher scheme as a means of ensuring the responsiveness of schools to the wishes of ethnic minority parents (Homan, 1986). Thirdly, the neoconservatives can be distinguished from their neoliberal counterparts in terms of the authoritarian-populist nature of their racial discourse. An important hallmark of the new racism has undoubtedly been its readiness to mobilize public opinion by appealing to the 'common sense' and to the 'genuine fears' of the British people. In contrast to the populist rhetoric of the neoconservatives, neoliberals have been more concerned to advocate the use of market forces to purge those irrational forms of economic discrimination and racial prejudice which may well be popular in society at large. Given the lack of ideological fit between the two contradictory strands within New Right race thinking, there would seem to be a convincing case for rejecting the very idea of a coherent and distinctive form of New Right race discourse.

Thatcherism and the politics of race

There can be little doubt that the Thatcher governments have failed to fulfil the expectations of many Conservative supporters in the area of race and immigration (Bulpitt, 1985) and that, as with other strands of Thatcherism, there is a gap between New Right rhetoric and the reality of New Right practice. There has been no radical break with the past. Many of the actions taken since 1979 represent either a development of earlier policies or a pragmatic response to immediate problems and pressures rather than the implementation of a new, well-defined Tory race strategy.

We insist that the main dimensions of the State's current response to race-related problems and issues were already well established when the first Thatcher Government took office. It is important to remember that throughout the 1960s and 1970s there had been a significant and steady shift to the right in British race politics. In particular, Powell's populist interventions on race had helped to foster the further development of tougher, racially discriminatory immigration controls. This process, overseen by successive Conservative and Labour governments, has been the dominant feature of State race policy since the early 1960s. Nevertheless, the impact of the racial message preached by Powell on State policy and practice should not be overestimated. The Powellite race offensive has conspicuously failed to undermine two other important features of British race politics that have continued to survive intact during the Thatcher era.

First, despite much vitriolic opposition from Powell and his allies, the Race Relations legislation, race QGAs and Government funded programmes (which together form the basis of the State's integrationist strategy), have not been seriously threatened. On the contrary, there is evidence that the 'race relations industry' has continued to grow since 1979, much of it sponsored directly or indirectly by central government. For example, various central government-financed special programmes inherited by the Thatcher administration (including the Urban Programme, a variety of Manpower Services Commission (MSC) initiatives and Section 11 of the Local Government Act 1966) have been increasingly used by some local authorities to fund special posts for work with ethnic minorities. Rather than 'rolling back' race-related spending programmes like Section 11, Conservtive governments have marginally increased its impact by widening the geographical areas and types of posts that can be funded under this provision (Ben-Tovim *et al.*, 1986). In this way, Thatcherism has actually facilitated the creation by local authorities of the very race relations advisers and special units so vehemently criticized by New Right intellectuals and the popular press.

Secondly, in spite of the concerted efforts of the New Right, race issues continue to occupy a marginal position on the national political agenda. Although race now has a higher profile in British politics – and certainly in the popular press – it has failed to become a major concern of central government. In reality, the Thatcher administrations have largely followed in the footsteps of their predecessors by off-loading prime responsibility for race matters onto other agencies (Bulpitt, 1985:133). Furthermore, this persistent political inaction on race and preference for 'colour-blind', racially inexplicit policies, can be seen as an indication of the dominance of certain neoliberal ideas within official race discourse, especially the typical liberal reluctance to treat individuals differently according to the group to which they belong (Jeffcoate, 1985). Here, at least, Thatcherism is best understood in terms of its continuity with the past. Successive governments have long been concerned to avoid policies that specifically address the problem of racial disadvantage or that may be seen to be of benefit to ethnic minorities. This has most obviously been the case with inner-city policies, which have traditionally avoided offering benefits exclusively to black communities living in areas of 'special need'. Instead, these communities are only able to benefit in a limited and indirect way from the allocation of resources to their urban area as a whole. Thatcherism has in practice only continued this trend.

In the sphere of race Thatcher governments, like their predecessors, have concentrated their efforts on intensifying the racist system of immigration controls.[3] Elsewhere, there has been no clear lead on race matters from central government. One consequence of this has been the loose, non-directive character of the limited central policy initiatives that have been produced (Ben-Tovim *et al.*, 1986). In particular, much has been deliberately left to the discretion of local authorities, who must decide whether and in what ways to make use of the opportunities available from central government. For example, Section 71 of the 1976 Race Relations Act requires local authorities to pursue an equal opportunities programme and Section 37 makes it possible for local organizations to take positive action to compensate for racial inequalities. Almost inevitably, this has led to the uneven development of race equality policies and equal opportunities programmes by local authorities, with significant variations existing not only between local authorities themselves but even between departments within the same authority (Ben-Tovim *et al.*, 1986:143). It would appear that Thatcherism has only served to foster an even more complex variety of local responses.

In reality, change in race policy and practice has originated more from inside the local state than from the impact of Thatcherite radicalism. These important changes have come from two distinct but overlapping sources. First, various professional groups such as teachers and social workers working within the State system have been important agents of innovation. One notable feature of this process has been the degree of discretion and collective autonomy that they have had over many years in shaping their own professional practice in race-related matters. In the past, both professions subscribed strongly to professional values that encouraged the adoption of colour-blind, universalist approaches to their work. Such thinking has been challenged in recent times from within the professions themselves by more racially explicit professional beliefs and practices (Coombe and Little, 1986). The resulting expansion of professionally initiated multicultural and anti-racist strategies has opened up these State professions to an intensified level of political scrutiny and ideological opposition, as well as to a considerable degree of internal debate and conflict.

Secondly, we need to take account of those local authority race initiatives which have emerged mainly since Mrs Thatcher took office. Municipal anti-racism represents the most open and arguably most serious challenge to the established methods of race management.[4] As such, it has sought both to redress the long-standing underdevelopment of race policy in Britain and to construct a new race politics in opposition to the broad policy stance of relative inaction and racial inexplicitness favoured by central government. In this sense, local authority initiatives have served to create a partial 'racialization' of policy (Troyna and Williams, 1986). An increasing proportion of social services departments and local education authorities have taken an overt stance on race, and more local authority provision has been targeted at the specific needs of black communities. For example, according to the Commission for Racial Equality, over 70 local authorities have so far launched anti-racist and multicultural policies as recommended by the Swann Report. In addition, a sizeable minority of 47 out of 115 local education authorities have published, or are working on, guidelines on racial harassment (O'Connor, 1988). More generally, it should be noted that many councils have taken up and belatedly exploited opportunities provided by existing race relations legislation and central government funding. Putting aside for the moment important questions concerning the quality and effectiveness of their implementation, there is a sharp contrast between the formation of new race policies at the level of the local state and the relative dearth of any new policy initiatives at the national level. This contrast is especially marked when it comes to comparing the response of central and local government to the urban riots of 1981 and 1985. The concerted effort advocated by Lord Scarman has failed to materialize and there has been no sign of any inter-departmental or Cabinet committee to lead 'the direct and co-ordinated attack on racial disadvantage' advocated in the Scarman Report (Prashar, 1987:115). This degree of political inaction illustrates well the failure of Thatcher governments to 'break the mould' in the politics of race. Instead, they have offered an increasingly tough law and order response to urban unrest, marked above all by their unconditional support for the police in developing new strategies for dealing with a supposedly criminal and riotous black population (Gilroy, 1987). In fact, the changes that have taken place in the policing of black communities illustrate precisely the way that subcentral agencies like the police are able to shape the State's response to race issues quite independently of any central political control. In effect, the role of government has been confined to supporting rather than steering the police's handling of race-related matters.

It is also abundantly clear that developments which have taken place in local race politics during the Thatcher years have triggered an escalating campaign against virtually all forms of anti-racism and multiculturalism. We believe that it is through the populist onslaught against anti-racism that the ideology of the New Right – especially in its social authoritarian form – can be seen to have had its most significant impact. The ideological campaign by the conservative-populist right in the area of race has taken a distinctively new turn in the 1980s. One vital change has been the widespread dissemination of New Right race-thinking within both the quality and tabloid sections of the British press (Murray, 1986). New Right intellectuals have increasingly been invited to express their views within the columns of the press, while at the same time race reporting in the post-1981 period has become more infected by the preoccupations of the new racism. This amplification and popularization of Powellite themes has affected race policy in at least two significant ways. First, media coverage of the 1981 and 1985 riots, in conjunction with the sensationalist reporting of 'street crime', has helped to set the agenda for subsequent policy debates over the policing of black communities (Murdock, 1984). In its reporting of riots and inner-city crime problems, the press has had an important effect on policing policy, particularly in terms of 'normalizing' the new styles of paramilitary policing. Secondly, the New Right popular press onslaught against anti-racism has worked to undermine the legitimacy of these anti-racist initiatives themselves by presenting them as being at one and the same time both ridiculous and menacing.

This campaign of 'anti-anti-racism' has undermined the legitimacy of the limited and tentative advances that have been made in the development of anti-racist policy and practice. In this sense, the impact of New Right ideology on race policy has been more negative than positive since it has served to curtail anti-racism rather than to foster the development of a distinctive set of New Right race policies. It is in terms of this process that we can make sense of some important recent developments in race policy and practice. First, there are some signs of a retreat from anti-racism on the part of local authorities. Most notably, Berkshire's much-praised 'model policy' on racial equality in education has recently been reconsidered by the Conservative-controlled county council, raising fears that this may well be the first of many such moves. Furthermore, Labour-controlled councils now appear somewhat less willing to pursue anti-racist policies in order to protect themselves against charges of 'loony leftism'.

Secondly, there have been a number of initiatives from central government which can be interpreted as part of an offensive against municipal anti-racism, as well as some indication of a belated attempt to erode the traditional pattern of local state autonomy in the area of race policy. For example, the wide-ranging assault that has been mounted by the Thatcher Government on local socialism has contained some specifically 'anti-anti-racist' components, such as the decision to outlaw almost totally the contract compliance policies favoured by some local authorities. More generally, the attack on local socialism has already claimed as victims the Greater London Council (GLC) and those other Metropolitan authorities who played a trail-blazing role in the development of equal opportunities and race equality programmes.

Finally, it is important to acknowledge the critical effect that the Education Reform Bill is likely to have on multicultural and anti-racist education policies (Saunders, 1988). The proposed open enrolment which is designed to give parents more choice is likely to leave many black parents with little choice but to have their children educated in largely black schools; the 'opting out' clause will give parents like those at Dewsbury, who are opposed to multicultural education, the chance to have their children educated in grant-maintained schools which will no longer be covered by Section 71 of the Race Relations Act; and the imposition of a national curriculum may well crowd out ethnic minority languages and other aspects of multicultural education from schools' timetables. Although the Education Reform Bill maintains the liberal tradition of racial inexplicitness that has characterized social policy making in Britain, there is no doubt that it represents an important setback for anti-racism and multiculturalism in schools. In the current political climate, with the social authoritarian New Right in full populist cry, what future can there be for anti-racist policy and practice?

Anti-racism in a cold climate

In recent years, anti-racism has had a bad press! Sections of the New Right, and in particular some of the tabloid newspapers, have been dramatically successful in mobilizing popular racist sentiments around campaigns of 'anti-anti-racism' which have made the task of developing policies to combat racism and racial disadvantage much more difficult. However, although the climate of public opinion has undoubtedly shifted against anti-racism, this can only in part be blamed on the political and ideological successes of the New Right. The failure to develop popular anti-racist initiatives has also been due to the over-zealous way in which these have often been implemented and to the ill-conceived nature of some of the policies themselves.

As far as the problem of the implementation of anti-racist policies is concerned, there has been a general failure to recognize that it is easier to be anti-racist in theory than in practice. In moving from the sphere of policy formulation to that of policy implementation, it is necessary to recognize that there are many areas where it is genuinely difficult to know in detail what anti-racist practice actually is. Of course there are times when it is necessary to 'stand up and be counted' on the issue of racism. But principled declarations of intent are never enough if they are not accompanied by serious consideration of the practical difficulties inherent in operationalizing them. We believe that the inability to establish a wider legitimacy for anti-racist initiatives is in part due to a failure to face up to these problems among committed anti-racists.

More generally, it is time to confront the uncomfortable fact that anti-racist policies have all too often been based upon assumptions and premises which are shared in common with sections of the New Right. Thus at times both racists and anti-racists have been critical of programmes designed to encourage the development of ethnic and cultural pluralism in society; both have generally been suspicious of the growth of the State-sponsored 'race relations industry'; and both have often adopted a common perspective on the central importance of culture in sustaining a sense of national identity. The struggle to move beyond Thatcherism in the sphere of race policy is therefore a struggle against ideas and assumptions that have considerable currency both on the right and left of British politics.

The debate over the issue of transracial fostering and adoption provides a good illustration both of the practical difficulties of implementing anti-racist policy declarations and of the dubious and questionable nature of some of these policies themselves. Some local authority social services departments (SSDs) have declared a ban on the practice of placing black children with white families for the purposes of fostering and adoption, on the grounds that this must inevitably engender identity confusion and poor self-esteem in the black child (Small, 1986). Failure to encourage the development of a positive black identity in such children will deprive them of one of the essential resources needed to survive in white-dominated racist society, it is argued.

There can be no disputing the fact that selection policies used by SSDs and adoption agencies have traditionally been distorted by the combined effects of racist, sexist and anglocentric assumptions concerning 'normal family life'. This has led to a serious under-representation of black families on the books of fostering and adoption agencies. Clearly defined policies designed to rectify this specific example of racial disadvantage are therefore a minimum requirement for all SSDs and adoption societies. However, in our view, this should not be accompanied by a blanket ban on the placement of black children with white families. In the first place, there are inevitably practical difficulties involved in the implementation of such a policy. Should social workers refuse to place black children with their older siblings who have previously been fostered with white families? Should they ignore the expressed preferences of young teenagers, especially those of mixed parentage, who choose to situate themselves predominantly within a white milieu? Above all, is it in the overall interests of the black child that s/he should remain in care solely because no black family is available or willing to accept the child? A policy decision that simply outlaws all transracial fostering and adoption is likely to lead to resentment and hostility among children and parents and above all among social workers who have to apply the policy in practice. The net effect will probably be to undermine the legitimacy of local authority anti-racist initiatives in general.

Secondly, this policy rests upon a highly questionable set of assumptions that have helped to shape and influence a range of anti-racist policies in recent years. Most obviously, there is the assumption that the family exercises a preponderent influence in the development of self-identity. No recognition is given to the role that may be played by the peer group, the school or the local community, particularly in those areas with a high proportion of black residents, in stimulating the development of a positive black identity. Neither is any thought given to possible ways of working with those white parents caring for black children so that they may be encouraged to foster rather than suppress their child's racial identity. Yet presumably it must be black youngsters in white homes who are most 'at risk' under a system which permits such transracial placements!

Ultimately, this position can only be sustained by falling back on a crude racial essentialism in which the categories of 'white' and 'black' are used in a simplistic and undifferentiated manner. The result has been that anti-racist policies – in the sphere of fostering and adoption, and elsewhere – have tended to assume that 'white = racist'. This belief is justified by appealing to the accumulated historical legacy of Empire, of slavery and of imperialism which it is argued has endowed our culture with a racism that is so deeply ingrained that today, all white people in Britain are inherently racist.

The disastrous and tragic effects of anti-racist policies that categorize the white community in this crude and undifferentiated way have been exposed most recently in the report of the inquiry into the murder of Ahmed Ullah at Burnage High School in Manchester.[5] The report says of anti-racist education:

> The basic assumption behind many policies is that since black students are the victims of the immoral and prejudiced behaviour of white students, white students are all to be seen as 'racist' whether

they are ferret-eyed fascists or committed anti-racists (quoted in Ward, 1988:2).

Thus, while the police refused to recognize that the murder had a racial dimension, the school and the local education authority decided that the killing was a cut-and-dried case of racism in which the whole white community were in effect collectively culpable. As a result, all white students, including Ahmed's friends, were prevented from attending the funeral and the report says that 'this helped to reinforce a feeling among white pupils that they were somehow to blame for the death' (*ibid.*). The consequence of this approach to anti-racist education was to polarize the Asian and white communities and to reinforce the very divisions that the policy was designed to overcome.

This narrow conception of the white community and white racism is mirrored in an equally simplistic view of the black community and of black resistance to racism, which are often defined in narrow 'culturalist' terms. In effect, culture is seen as the prime determinant of racial identity which is equated with an almost mystical notion of 'blackness'. The corollary of this is a form of anti-racist politics that is racially exclusive and that draws its inspiration from certain strands of black nationalism (Gilroy, 1987:65).

The first and most obvious objection to this position is that, in the British context, it offers to the black community a form of politics which has little or no chance of winning concrete political gains. Of course, in common with other forms of political mythology, black cultural nationalism undoubtedly provides a potent source of powerful images that can from time to time galvanize sections of the black underclass into mass political action. But mythologies can also induce a sense of frustration and resignation, precisely because they hold out the promise of Utopian solutions that are quite unrealizable in practice. While it may be appropriate elsewhere, Britain's black population is far too small to engage successfully in forms of nationalist politics that are racially/culturally exclusive. Strategically , black cultural nationalism represents not the politics of the ghetto but the politics of the cul-de-sac.

The second objection to the idealized conception of black culture that has informed many recent anti-racist initiatives is that it fails to give adequate attention to the diversity of interests that are present within Britain's black community. The tendency to 'read off' anti-racist policies from simplistic notions of black culture fails to recognize that different sections of the black community may not necessarily be in agreement over anti-racist priorities. The gradual expansion of the Asian business class, for example, or the emergence of an independent black feminist movement illustrates the diversity of interests among the black population in contemporary Britain. Unless these different interests are adequately represented in the formulation of anti-racist initiatives, they will not command the broad support of those whose needs they are designed to meet.

Thirdly, and most seriously, the culturalist conception of racial identity that underlies the theory and practice of much contemporary anti-racism is strikingly similar to the ideas of 'belongingness' and 'nationhood' that are current on the social authoritarian wing of the New Right (Gilroy, 1987). Paradoxically, sections of the new urban left have reproduced a form of reasoning that connects a unitary conception of culture to group identity and to a racially exclusive form of politics. Here 'right' and 'left' thinking on race and racism coexist in a symbiotic relationship in which each is the mirror image of the other. In the one, black culture is dismissed as pathological and is seen as a potential threat to a 'British way of life' that is consecrated in cultural terms. In the other, black culture is celebrated as a robust and vital 'culture of resistance' capable of sustaining black people in their struggles against a white society that is in turn pathologized as irredeemably racist. What links the two is the common elision of national/racial identity and culture and the shared tendency to treat the category of culture in a thoroughly ahistorical manner.

Given these shared assumptions, it is perhaps not surprising to find that sections of the new urban left and the New Right have found yet more common ground in their rejection of the philosophy of multiculturalism, particularly as it has been developed within the education system. Following the canonization of the ex-Bradford headmaster Ray Honeyford in some sections of the popular press, there has been a sustained attack by individuals on the social authoritarian wing of the New Right against the whole idea of multicultural education (Palmer, 1986). However, opposition to the idea of multiculturalism does not come only from sections of the New Right. Some black radicals have also been critical of the philosophy underpinning multicultural education in schools, seeing it at best as a diversionary tactic designed to focus attention away from the serious under-resourcing of inner-city schools (Stone, 1981) or at worst a strategy designed to contain and control the incipient revolt of the black underclass (Dhondy et al., 1982). The result has been that debate on the left has tended to polarize around 'multiculturalism' vs 'anti-racism' (Troyna and Williams, 1986). In our view, the attempt to present these as fundamentally opposed is a mistake. In particular, we wish to argue in favour of some aspects of multiculturalism, especially since we believe that these can assist in the task of winning a wider consent for anti-racist policies which can thereby be implemented all the more successfully.

The problem is that multiculturalism is a movable feast, meaning different things to different people. We reject completely the 'theory' of multiculturalism that identifies it as a means of eradicating the poorly developed self-concept that most black people are supposed to have of themselves. Such an approach is fundamentally racist since it is based upon false and misleading assumptions concerning the pathological nature of the black family and black culture. On the other hand, there is nothing racist in the idea that everyone should be encouraged to learn about and respect the cultural diversity of their society. In particular, the school environment is one where children can be encouraged to appreciate and enjoy the positive benefits of cultural differences and where multicultural education, properly conceived, can be used to break down some of the worst excesses of anglocentrism that are still rampant in many schools. On its own, multiculturalism is not enough. It needs to be located within a broader framework of anti-racist policies and initiatives designed to address the problems of racial discrimination and disadvantage. Therefore, ethnic and racial monitoring by agencies and institutions, coupled with the rigorous promotion of equal opportunities policies, are among the measures needed to provide a firm anti-racist foundation for multiculturalism.

It is above all the market liberal wing of the New Right who tend to be suspicious of these kinds of State-sponsored initiatives that are designed to foster 'forced equality'. The standard argument against all such initiatives, which as we have shown has received less attention in Britain than in the USA, is that the unintended consequences of such policies always produce outcomes that are worse than the initial problems. The real beneficiaries of State-funded programmes designed to alleviate disadvantages are either the middle classes, who somehow manage to hijack the resources for themselves, or the State bureaucrats who misuse these resources to engage in 'empire building', thereby enhancing their own power and prestige inside the State. In either case it is the targeted group – the poor, the blacks, or whoever – who lose out.

However, opposition to the idea of State-sponsored anti-racism and suspicion of those who advocate or actively promote this is not confined to the New Right. Many on the left have been highly critical of the so-called 'race relations industry' which is sometimes seen as part of a Machiavellian plot designed to create 'a class of coloured collaborators who would in time justify the ways of the State to the blacks' (Sivanandan, 1976).

More recent evidence suggests that at a local level, a variety of State policies in the spheres of race, local government, education, the inner city and employment have created a considerable degree of political 'space' within which successful and popular anti-racist strategies can be developed (Ben-Tovim *et al.*, 1986). Of course, there can be no guarantee that effective policies will automatically result from each and every attempt to exploit these opportunities. In particular, it is necessary to campaign vigorously against the imposition of 'top-down' forms of anti-racism that are initiated at the level of the local state without the involvement of local communities in their formulation and implementation. In the absence of such democratic participation, State-sponsored anti-racism is likely to reproduce many of the unacceptable racist assumptions that have all too frequently been a feature of such policies in the past. Nevertheless, in spite of the risks involved, we totally reject the claim made by sections of the radical left that effective anti-racism can only be pursued outside the confines of the State.

Neither can we subscribe to the view that the market, if left to itself, will automatically eliminate racial discrimination and disadvantage. The argument that employers and others will only cease to discriminate against blacks and other disadvantaged groups when it becomes too costly for them to continue to do so, can in fact be used to justify more rather than less State intervention to secure racial equality. Market liberals have always believed that individual market transactions should take place within a framework of law enacted and enforced by the State. Presumably, individuals are deterred from breaking the law in the pursuit of their self-interest because to do so is likely to be 'too costly' for them in terms of fines or possible imprisonment. The same argument can be used to support a considerable strengthening of the legal framework designed to combat racial disadvantage. Such a framework might include some or all of the following: measures to require ethnic monitoring in all firms and agencies; equal opportunities requirements in the spheres of recruitment, training and promotion; and provisions for forms of contract compliance. Firms and individuals would then be able to weigh up the opportunity costs of not complying with the law – and 'market forces' would discipline those who made the wrong choice!

Such an argument illustrates very clearly the futility of any attempt to polarize 'State *vs* market' in any simplistic way. Since the pursuit of self-interest is never an unconditional freedom but is always constrained by a framework of law, the New Right cannot dispense with the State. It is then a question of deciding on the proper role and function of the State and, in particular, on the extent to which the State should act so as to curb 'consumer preferences'. We favour a far more extensive framework of legal and administrative rules designed to promote racial equality, together with a substantial increase in resources devoted to their implementation.[6] As we have already made clear, this strategy runs the risk of amplifying the racism that is already institutionalized within State policy and provision. Nevertheless, we believe that the elimination of racial discrimination and disadvantage is far more likely to be achieved through an increase in State intervention rather than through the operation of the free market.

Notes

1   These are mainly contained in the publications of the libertarian Institute of Economic Affairs, though a brief discussion can be found in *The 'New Right' Enlightenment* (Seldon, 1985) and in the similarly titled volume of essays that accompanied the Channel Four television series (Graham and Clarke, 1986).
2   For a fuller discussion of the competing social authoritarian and market liberal viewpoints on race, see Mitchell and Russell (forthcoming).
3   Though it is worth noting that some of the harsher measures contained in the 1979 Conservative election manifesto have not in fact been enacted.
4   The term municipal anti-racism is taken from Gilroy (1987).
5   At the time of writing the report has still to be published. Therefore, we have had to rely on the extensive media coverage that has been given to the report in the 'quality' daily and weekly press.
6   The Commission for Racial Equality, which operates within a framework of extensive legal powers, has never been allocated the resources necessary to put these powers to good effect in combating racism.

References

Ashford, N. (1985). The bankruptcy of collectivism. In *The 'New Right' Enlightenment* (A. Seldon, ed.), pp. 33–45. Sevenoaks: Economic and Literary Books.

Barker, M. (1981). *The New Racism*. London: Junction Books.

Ben-Tovim, G., Gabriel, J., Law, I. and Stredder, K. (1986). *The Local Politics of Race*. London: Macmillan.

Bulpitt, J. (1985). Continuity, autonomy and peripheralisation: The anatomy of the centre's statecraft in England. *Environment and Planning C: Government and Policy*, **3**, 129–47.

Centre for Contemporary Cultural Studies (1982). *The Empire Strikes Back*. London: Hutchinson.

Coombe, V. and Little, A. (eds) (1986). *Race and Social Work: A Guide to Training*. London: Tavistock.

Daljord, M. (1985). American second-generation immigrant. In *The 'New Right' Enlightenment* (A. Seldon, ed.), pp. 213–23. Sevenoaks: Economic and Literary Books.

Davies, S. (1985). Sources and Origins. In *The 'New Right' Enlightenment* (A. Seldon, ed.), pp. 33–45. Sevenoaks: Economic and Literary Books.

Dhondy, F., Beese, B. and Hassan, L. (1982). *The Black Explosion in British Schools*. London: Race Today Publications.

Gilroy, P. (1987). *There Ain't No Black in the Union Jack*. London: Hutchinson.

Gordon, P. and Klug, F. (1986). *New Right, New Racism*. London: Searchlight.

Graham, D. and Clarke, P. (1986). *The New Enlightenment: The Rebirth of Liberalism*. London: Macmillan.

Homan, R. (1986). Ethnic minorities reject the remote State. *Economic Affairs*, April/May, 26–9.

Jeffcoate, R. (1985). Anti-racism as an educational ideology. In *Race and Gender: Equal Opportunities Policies in Education* (M. Arnot, ed.), pp. 53–63. Oxford: Pergamon Press.

Majewski, J. (1988). The economics of race and discrimination. *Economic Affairs,* February/March, 23–9.

Mitchell, M. and Russell, D. (forthcoming). *Immigrants and Minorities).*

Murdock, G. (1984). Reporting the riots: Images and impact. In *Scarman and After* (J. Benyon, ed.), pp. 73–95. Oxford: Pergamon Press.

Murray, N. (1986). Anti-racists and other demons: The press and ideology in Thatcher's Britain. *Race and Class,* **XXVII**(3), 1–19.

O'Connor, M. (1988). A move in the wrong direction. *Education Guardian,* 5 April, p. 21.

Palmer, F. (ed.) (1986). *Anti-racism: An Assault on Education and Value.* London: Sherwood.

Prashar, U. (1987). Too much talk and not enough positive action. In *The Roots of Urban Unrest* (J. Benyon and J. Solomos, eds), pp. 115–18. Oxford: Pergamon Press.

Saunders, C. (1988). Baker's bill: Education for all? *New Society, Race and Society Supplement,* 5 February, pp. 2–3.

Seldon, A. (ed.) (1985). *The 'New Right' Enlightenment.* Sevenoaks: Economic and Literary Books.

Sivanandan, A. (1976). Race, class and the State: The black experience in Britain. *Race and Class,* **XVII**(4), 347–68.

Small, J. (1986). Transracial placements: Conflicts and contradictions. In *Social Work with Black Children and their Families* (S. Ahmed, J. Cheetham and J. Small, eds). London: Batsford.

Sowell, T. (1983). *The Economics and Politics of Race: An International Perspective.* New York: William Morrow.

Stone, M. (1981). *The Education of the Black Child in Britain.* London: Fontana.

Troyna, B. and Williams, J. (1986). *Racism, Education and the State.* London: Croom Helm.

Ward, D. (1988). Failed race policy that left out whites. *The Guardian,* 28 April.

Williams, W. (1982). *The State Against Blacks.* New York: McGraw Hill.

6 The Family

Pamela Abbott and Claire Wallace

Introduction

The idea of the family has been an essential part of Thatcherite social and economic policy. Politicians frequently assert that they are supporting family life and this immediately strikes a sympathetic and sentimental chord; everyone wants to defend 'the family'. But what exactly is 'the family' and how do the facts of the case relate to the rhetorical claim?

The commonsense definition of a family is that it is a heterosexual couple unit based upon monogamous legal marriage in which children are raised. It is seen as the 'natural' domestic unit – the way in which people *ought* to live. However, such a model of the family can be shown to be an ideology and one which does not describe the domestic arrangements of most people in contemporary Britain.

It was not until the (mostly feminist) writings of the 1960s and 1970s that this ideological concept was seriously challenged. In this critique, it became evident that the family was not a 'natural' or 'universal' domestic arrangement and that our Western nuclear family was fairly atypical both historically and in comparison with other cultures (Gittins, 1985). Moreover, this conception of domestic living is being challenged by many common social practices. Although the majority of people may have lived in a family at some point in their lives, in fact only a small minority of households consist of a married couple with male breadwinner and dependent wife and children (at any one time). Households consisting of a single person, non-married couples and single parents have all increased dramatically over the last 10 years (Office of Population Censuses and Surveys, 1988). For those who do live as couples, some have already been married at least once before, and the majority of women work for a good part of the time that they are so-called 'homemakers'. Hence, if the family is the natural and universal form of domestic arrangement, this is not reflected in the way in which people actually construct households. In this sense, then, it would make more sense to talk about 'households' than 'families'. However, in terms of the model which people may hold as ideal it still makes sense to talk about 'the family' as an ideology. In this article, therefore, we will talk of 'the family' as an ideology, but 'families' will be used to refer to domestic arrangements consisting of couples with children, while recognizing that this does not cover all the different types of households.

Although the members of Mrs Thatcher's Government have no explicit family policy as such, they do hold a particular image of 'the family' and this we can glean from speeches, journalism and policy statements. Here we will discuss the way in which this has influenced the impact which the policies of the Conservative administration since 1979 has had on families. There are a number of different strands of thought within the New Right which would construct the family differently. Indeed, there has been a profusion of ideas emerging from quarters such as the Centre for Policy Studies, the Adam Smith Institute, as well as individual writers such as Johnson, Mount, Scruton and the so-called 'moral right' (various religious groups, the anti-abortion lobby, etc.). However, it is not clear to what extent these views are shared by Conservatives actually in office.

Consequently, we will concentrate mainly upon policy documents and manifestos produced since 1979. We will argue that in fact at least some of the New Right have been highly critical of Government policies – or lack of them – on the family and that some of this criticism comes from within the Conservative Party itself. We will then examine the impact that policies implemented under Thatcher have had on the family: we will do this by looking at policies explicitly aimed at the family and at policies that have not been seen as directly concerned with the family, but nevertheless have implications for 'families'. We will conclude with an analysis of alternative family policies.

The New Right ideology of the family

It is important to recognize that the ideology of the family has always played a central role in social and economic policy – at least since the early nineteenth century. Indeed, it can be argued that the British State has always served to create and sustain a particular type of family – the patriarchal nuclear family described above. This idea of the family underpinned the legislation that laid down the foundations of the

Welfare State after the Second World War. In Beveridge's view, the role of the State was to protect the family, which is primarily responsible for welfare. Vulnerable people – like women and children – would need support only if for some reason they fell out of the confines of the family, such as through widowhood. Otherwise, the family would provide the social and financial support for its members through the male breadwinner's connection with the labour market (Beveridge, 1942). State intervention, however, was encouraged in order to ensure the proper conformity of family life through the agency of health visitors, social workers and so on.

This view of the family, however, rapidly became unworkable. The rising numbers of women going out to work meant that the role of housewife was no longer a woman's sole occupation after marriage. With rising rates of divorce and illegitimacy, women and children were often dependent upon State supplementary benefits, rather than being supported by the family. The growing numbers of elderly people, mostly State dependents, and the increasing tendency for young people to leave home and set up separate households without being married, has also led to demands upon the housing benefits and supplementary benefits system. These changes in family life are, in part, what have led to the huge rise in benefit spending as a proportion of the Government's total expenditure. Hence, the Conservative administration elected in 1979 argued that some review of social security was required in the light of these and other changes in the social structure.

The New Right's view of the family differs from Beveridge's in so far as it makes reference back to an imputed 'traditional' family which existed before State interventionism and State support started to undermine it:

> It is time to change the approach to what Governments can do for people and what people can do for themselves. Time to shake off the self-doubt induced by decades of dependence on the state as master not servant (Mrs Thatcher's speech to the Conservative Party Conference, 1979).

For the New Right, the family has a number of different uses. On the one hand, it could be a convenient way of saving money for the national exchequer – by re-emphasizing the financial responsibility of the family – but it is also a way of solving various social problems. Hence, under Thatcherism, there are explicit statements about the importance of the family to society and an emphasis on its moral responsibilities. It is argued that the decline in the importance of marriage and the family is a major cause of Britain's current social and economic problems. The State, it is argued, has taken away rights and responsibilities from parents, has permitted families to lose their independence, while legislative changes on abortion and divorce have permitted a decline in moral values and the perceived importance of the family. This decline in parental authority as a consequence of the decline in family values generally is at the root of many social problems associated with threats to the dominant moral order:

> The origins of crime lie deep in society: in families where parents do not support or control their children, in schools where discipline is poor; and in the wider world where violence is glamourised and traditional values are under attack (Conservative Party manifesto, 1987:55).

And, 'It's at home that children first learn right from wrong' (speech by Mrs Thatcher, 1985).

Hence, the problems of the inner city will be solved not only by Government spending but

> by bringing back personal responsibility (through ownership), security (through law and order) and stability (through strengthening a sense of personal obligation, most notably within families) (Tebbit, 1985).

In part, at least, this can be viewed as a moral counterbalance, an attack on the permissiveness of the 1960s, the rise of gay liberation, the women's movement and changes in styles of domestic living. It can also be seen as a re-statement of traditional conservative views of the family and its centrality as a social institution – a view that social change has gone too far and that social and economic order will break down if the patriarchal family is not established as the norm. In the words of Paul Johnson (1982):

> The ideal society must rest upon the tripod of a strong family, a voluntary church and a liberal, minimum state. The family is the most important.

This view of the family, deriving from Christian morality, is that it should be based upon marriage: 'The family is formed by the institution of marriage which is a union for life and is the vital link which binds together the family' (Conservative Political Centre, 1981:28). Thus it is developments such as the women's movement which have challenged the traditional, biologically ordained division of labour between men and women. In the now famous words of Patrick Jenkin in 1977:

Quite frankly, I don't think that mothers have the same right to work as fathers do. If the good Lord had intended us to have equal rights to go out to work he wouldn't have created men and women. These are biological facts.

Also contained in this rhetoric is a concern with giving families more rights, responsibilities and choice – over housing, for example, and over education by enhancing the power of parents over teachers (cf. Brown, Chapter 3, this volume).

A number of problems arise with this perspective. If one type of family is prioritized, how does this affect other types of domestic arrangement? This view assumes a consensus on 'the family' as being the natural and normal way to live, which does not in fact exist. This view of the family also contains a number of contradictory strands. On the one hand, the ideas derived from economic liberalism given the importance attached to the free individual, unfettered by the burdens of red tape, bureaucracy and State surveillance. This view derives from classical models of the labour market, such as those of Adam Smith. The logical implications of this view are that individuals should be allowed to pursue their self-interest by forming whatever sexual liaisons take their fancy, by consuming whatever product the marketplace has to offer them unhindered by State restrictions on pornography, and by getting divorced when they choose to. Indeed, the logical extension of economic liberalism is the fragmentation of the family, for why should a self-interested individual support a lot of dependents? The traditional conservative view of the family on the other hand, is that it is a seat of patriarchal authority, not individual self-interest, and that family members have responsibility to take care of each other. This contradiction is reconciled by constantly referring to the phrase 'individuals and their families' which allows them to be presented as a united set of interests as in: 'We shall continue to return more choice to individuals and their families' (Conservative Party, 1983).

This view of the family assumes that it represents a united set of interests in other ways too, by ignoring the important fact that not all members of the family may experience it in the same way, and that there is a dark side to family life in the form of the sexual and physical abuse of wives and children and the unequal division of power, labour and resources within the home. There is a further implicit contradiction between the need to promote maximum economic efficiency in the economy and the traditional morality of the family. Thus, for example, the Conservative view of the family appears to be one where women stay at home and yet the drive for profitability and low wages means that Britain has more married women in the labour force than any other European nation and this trend has increased since the Conservatives came into office.

Equally important, however, we shall argue that Conservative Government policies have actually done little to help the family even in their own terms. We suggest that their policies have actually undermined the ability of some families to care for and take on responsibility for their members and that much of the rhetoric concerning the family is actually designed to shift the cost of the support of children and other dependents away from the State.

Thatcherite family policy

The Conservative Party regards itself as 'the party of the family', in the 1983 Conservative Party manifesto, for example, five 'great tasks' are identified, one of which was 'to build a responsible society which protects the weak but allows the family and the individual to flourish'. Mrs Thatcher has also made it clear that her policies should be tested against their impact on the family: 'We shall judge these policies by one simple test: do they make life better for individuals and their families?' (New Year Message, 30 December 1983).

How far have they succeeded? On the one hand, they have introduced various measures which are recognized as supporting the family by the Moral Right, e.g. Clause 29 of the Local Government Act 1988 which prevents local authorities from 'promoting homosexuality', and the clause of the Education Act 1986 which requires that sex education be taught in the context of heterosexual family values. A further apparent victory for the Moral Right has been the reversal of the so-called 'tax on marriage', with the 1988 Budget removing some of the tax advantages enjoyed by those who cohabit rather than marry.

However, the formation of the Conservative Party Family Campaign (CPFC) in March 1986, can be seen as implicit criticism of the Party leadership and an indication that not all Conservatives think that the Conservative Government has done much to support the family and its values:

> What we are concerned with today is setting in motion a movement which will bring the family back into a position of strength in society. The family must be placed once more at the centre of society. The people best equipped to supervise and guide the young are two parents, committed to each other in marriage, who feel confident in their position as prime carers for their children (Dr David Amess, MP for Basildon, at the Launch of the CPFC on 17 March 1986).

More recently, Paul Johnson has argued that Mrs Thatcher's regime has lacked the will to change policies on the family. Echoing the arguments of the CPFC, he points to specific moral and economic failings, specifically the moral line taken in the AIDS advertising campaign and the Government's 'failure to give support to the family'. Furthermore, he argues that much Government policy harms the family:

> The lack of a family policy is a devastating hole in the heart of modern Conservatism. Nobody is asking the Government to extend its responsibilities. The truth is that it is already involved. In countless different ways government – central and local – has an impact on the family: through the tax law, rating policy, housing, health, education. The cumulative influence of all these forms of interference at present operates against family stability (Johnson, 1987:12).

The consequences of Thatcherite policy for families

It is evident that there is considerable disquiet about the extent to which Mrs Thatcher has headed a 'Government of the Family'. Certainly, there has been much rhetoric, but in practice little has been done to prioritize the 'traditional' family and to reduce family disintegration or dependency on the State. This is probably at least partly because it is difficult for politicians to put such ideas into practice. However, it is arguable that some Thatcherite policies may actually have weakened the family's ability to take on responsibility for its members and increased rather than reduced dependence on the State. This is because traditional Conservative beliefs about the family are combined with a commitment to inequality, which is regarded as essential to generate the competition and initiative necessary to a flourishing market. Thus the emphasis on the self-reliance of the family becomes important on economic as well as moral grounds. Indeed, the family is the lynchpin which holds together the public world of economics and the private world of 'traditional' morality. It is also evident that even if she sympathizes with their aims, Mrs Thatcher has not – with a few notable exceptions – listened to the pleas of the Moral Right. Furthermore, as we shall show, if we take literally Mrs Thatcher's suggestion that her policies should 'make life better for individuals and their families', we can demonstrate that she has failed.

The emphasis of the Conservative Government has been upon making families more self-reliant in catering for the welfare of sick or dependent family members rather than relying on the State:

> If we are to sustain, let alone extend, the level and standard of care in the community, we must first try to put the responsibility back where it belongs, with the family and with people themselves (Thatcher, 1977:83).

Not only are families seen as the natural units for providing such care, but cuts in public welfare spending on dependent groups, together with the closure of institutions means that there is little alternative. Much of the burden falls upon the women who are expected to take on the caring role. These policies take no account of the load which care places on untrained women who are expected to provide it for 24 hours per day, 7 days a week, and no account of the costs. Research has shown that caring for a dependent relative places an economic burden on the family, even allowing for the benefits received (Buckle, 1984). Furthermore, many women are forced to give up paid employment, thus lowering the family's standard of living. Similarly, changes in policies for youth, such as making Youth Training Schemes (YTS) compulsory for all 16- and 17-year-olds and reducing benefits for those under the age of 26 (by the Social Security Act 1986, implemented in April 1988), have increased the reliance of young people on the economic support of their parents.

Housing policy has also failed to meet the needs of many families. The emphasis on home ownership has left many unable to meet mortgage repayments; mortgage foreclosures have more than quadrupled since 1979 (Office of Population Censuses and Surveys, 1988). This, together with the sale of council housing and spiralling costs for private-sector rented housing, has left many families homeless; at Christmas, 1987, it was estimated that 250,000 children were without homes (Brimacombe, 1987). In other areas, the Government's attempts to reduce spending on welfare benefits have reduced the ability of families to provide for themselves. Cuts in educational spending have meant that schools need to rely increasingly on parents for the provision of books and equipment and that parents have to pay for 'extras' such as music, swimming lessons and field trips. Similar cuts in the real level of student grants have put an increased financial burden on parents. Reductions in health and social service spending also put pressure on families, with longer queues and waiting lists and a lack of beds and other resources for operations. Prescription charges, for example, have increased by 1100% since 1979, along with increased charges for spectacles and dental care, and this creates further economic burdens for families who have to deal with health and education for a number of dependents.

Since 1979 male unemployment has risen dramatically, while Government policies have made it more attractive for employers to take on part-time female (married) workers. Unemployment forces the family on to State benefits, and Government policy has been to shift the emphasis from insurance-based benefits, with the removal of earnings-related supplements, towards means-tested benefits, which they argue are targeted at those most in need. Meanwhile, the universal Child Benefit has been allowed to decline in value.

The real impact of Tory policies has been on poorer families, who are considerably worse off. The intention has been to target benefits at those in need, thus presumably increasing self-reliance and self-esteem among others. Under the new Social Security Act this situation will be exacerbated: in the illustrative figures which have been given, a family with two children with an income of £100 or less per week will be worse off, in some cases by as much as £11 per week because of reductions in housing benefit and free school meals (*Hansard*, 1986). Some will gain from the new regulations and some will lose, but the main effect will be to redistribute benefits *among the poor*. Despite the fact that the 'Family Credit' and the 'Family Premium' are aimed specifically at families, they do not consistently advantage 'traditional' nuclear families over other family forms.

Similarly, taxation policies have not been designed unambiguously to direct resources towards the family. Since 1979 the Conservatives have reduced income tax substantially, from a standard rate of 33p in the pound to 25p, and reduced the higher tax bands to a single rate of 40p in the pound. However, they have also raised National Insurance contributions and Value Added Tax (VAT). The net result has been to increase the tax burden on the lowest paid and to decrease it for the highest paid – the hardest hit of all being the married man with two children on half the national male average earnings, whose tax and National Insurance contributions increased by 163% between 1978 and 1987–8, compared with a 1% increase for a man on male average earnings and 21% decrease for a man earning ten times the national average (this is before the changes brought about by the 1988 Budget). When other factors such as VAT, changes in rates and the imputed benefits of Government spending on services, health and benefits are taken into account, a similar picture emerges. The income shared by the bottom 20% of households has declined by 9% and that of the bottom 40% by 7%, whereas the income of the top 40% of households has increased by 3% and that of the top 20% by 6% (Byrne, 1987).

Rather than the family being somehow proudly autonomous, we can see that its roles and relations, its responsibilities and tasks, and most of all its finances, are all determined by State policy, although mostly indirectly. Moreover, it appears to us that, despite the arguments of the Moral Right and the way in which this discourse has been used by Mrs Thatcher (although, interestingly enough, she does not herself follow the domestic career laid down for women by the Moral Right), the policies of familial responsibility have largely been taken on board as a means of saving money rather than out of moral concern.

While Mrs Thatcher appears to share the concern of the Moral Right over the apparent failure of the patriarchal family to assert itself and the traditional conservative view that the family is a basic building block of society, her policies have done little in practice to change the ways in which the State relates to families. Policies have continued to prioritize the heterosexual nuclear family and in some cases to reinforce the view that this is the only morally correct living arrangement, thus reinforcing familial ideology. The necessity to strengthen the family's sense of responsibility for its own welfare, by reducing intervention and reliance on the Welfare State, has been accompanied, we have argued, by a reduction in the economic ability of many families to do just that. Many families and individuals have had their ability to care for themselves *reduced*, not increased, by Thatcherite policies: the choices available to families are determined by income, which for many families has been reduced in real terms.

Thatcherite policies have been criticized both by the Moral Right, for failing to 'bring back' the patriarchal family, and by the centre and left, for increasing the economic and social burdens placed on families. Feminists, gay groups and the libertarian left have been more critical still; they argue that Thatcherite policies have reduced individual choices by asserting that there is only one acceptable domestic living arrangement and continuing to assume (as previous governments have done) that people not only do live in nuclear families but ought to do so. Alternative ways of living become difficult to choose, not only because of economic and social policies, but because of the ways in which familial ideology is constantly reinforced, making alternative living arrangements seem not only less desirable, but deviant or even morally wrong.

Alternative family policies

The family policies of the Conservative Party, then, have been premised on the view that there is one and only one acceptable family form and that Government policies should be directed to supporting and sustaining this form of family. However, we have argued that the policies of the Conservative Government, while increasing the responsibilities of families, have failed to provide the necessary support, especially for poor families.

It seems to us that there are two alternative sets of policies that could arguably overcome the problems of existing ones. The first of these, that policies should be tested against the criteria of family support, has been put forward by both the left and the right. The second, often referred to as 'deaggregation', would be to accept on the one hand that people live in a variety of household types, not privileging one form over any other and, on the other, to recognize that the interests of individual family members cannot necessarily be 'read off' from the interests of the family as a whole.

The provision of a 'family audit' would ensure that all legislation was scrutinized for the impact it would have on families, and that legislation that would have an adverse impact was rejected or amended as necessary. This position has been argued, for example, by Patrick Jenkin, who suggested:

> Ministers would be asked to accompany any new proposals with an account of their impact on the family. In this way Parliament, Cabinet and the people can be vigilant to safeguard and enhance the quality of family life (quoted in Craven *et al.* 1982:35).

The Family Policy Studies Centre has advanced similar arguments, while the Labour Party has suggested that there should be a Minister for the Family with a government department responsible for overseeing family policy.

While it is not inevitable, the danger of such policies is that they will fail, as policies based on patriarchal ideologies of the family do, to recognize that different members of a family have different and often conflicting needs, that most households do *not* constitute a family, and that legislation and legal rights do not guarantee that individuals or families will be able to make desired choices. We would suggest that policies have to be based on a number of key principles:

1   That people should be able to choose how they live, so that alternatives to the existing favoured patterns of family life should become realistically available.
2   That the needs of individual family members have to be seen as important.
3   That, none the less, for the foreseeable future, most men and women will continue to marry and have children and want to live in 'conventional' families.
4   That State intervention is necessary both to protect the rights of family members and to ensure that everyone has access to basic services and resources.
5   That most households do not comprise nuclear families and that prioritizing families can disadvantage those who do not choose to or cannot live in such families, e.g. the elderly.

The major policies that follow from these points relate both to the removal of legislation that discriminates against those who do not live in conventional families, and the active promotion of equal rights and equal opportunities legislation, so that, for example, individuals have the opportunity to obtain employment that pays a wage sufficient for them to live on and to have access to good, affordable housing. Prioritizing the needs of families has meant, for example, that the housing needs of single people and couples have been ignored in the public sector.

In the same way, families and their individual members must have the right to make realistic choices and the resources needed to support these choices. Thus good, affordable housing should be available for all families as of right. Women should not only have the right to choose whether or not to have children, but they should have access to good, free contraception advice, abortion facilities and maternity services. Similarly, mothers should have the realistic choice of whether or not they want to take paid employment. This means that there should be adequate, affordable nursery places for all mothers who want their children to go there, and preschool play-group provision for all mothers who prefer to stay at home with their children for part of the day. (On the other hand, mothers must respect the right of their children to have preschool education and take part in activities outside the home.) Similarly, after-school activities should be provided for all children who want to participate or whose parents want them to participate. Income support should be provided to all mothers so that they are not economically dependent on their partners and so that the decision to work or not is a genuine choice and not based on economic necessity. State policies must also recognize that marriages do break up, that some men are violent to their wives and that, for whatever reason, some single parents are left to bring up children on their own. Economic support from the State should mean that women do not to have to remain economically dependent on their ex-partners. Refuges should be provided by government; there should be enough places to provide for all women who seek help, and their standard should be high. Women who wish to leave a violent partner should be provided with good housing and legal protection. The police should have a legal duty to prosecute men who assault their wives, and women assaulted by their partners should be offered counselling and support. These would seem to be the bare minimum of provisions that follow from a serious attempt to meet the separate needs of men, women, children and families.

Finally, State policies should recognize the needs and rights of children in their own right and not assume that parents 'naturally' love and care for their children and want to provide the best for them. The needs of children must be prioritized and recognition given that children are relatively powerless and can make few choices for themselves. The State must take on the responsibility for actively promoting the welfare of all children rather than merely intervening when something is found to have gone wrong. Children should have a right not only to be fed, clothed, generally cared for and not physically or sexually assaulted, but also to have access to preschool education and a wide range of extracurricular activities. Access to the latter at present depends not only on parents' willingness to facilitate their children's participation but also on their parents having the means to pay for them. Such activities should be provided for all children, free at the point of presentation.

The policies for which we would argue, then, are designed not only to give individuals equal rights, however they may choose to live, but also provide the ability to exercise choice: ability to pay, the willingness of the wage-earner to share the 'family wage', the gate-keeping activities of doctors, social workers, housing officers and employers – these should not hinder or prevent people exercising their right to make choices. While the ultimate hope is that familial discourse will cease to be dominant – because it is a discourse which constrains choices and privileges some forms of living arrangement over others – short-term policy objectives must be to resist the discourse by ensuring that, on the one hand, the needs of individuals are not subsumed under assumed needs of families and, on the other, that people who are not in families are not disadvantaged or ignored because of the prioritization of the family.

Acknowledgements

We would like to thank Martin Loney and Roger Sapsford of the Open University Press for directing us to material for this chapter.

References

Beveridge, W. (1942). Report of the Committee on Social Insurance and Allied Services (Beveridge Committee). London: HMSO.

Brimacombe, M. (1987). *Where Homeless Now?* London: Shelter.

Buckle, J. (1984). *Mental Handicap Costs More.* London: Disablement Income Group.

Byrne, D. (1987). Rich and poor: The growing divide. In *The Growing Divide: A Social Audit 1979–1987* (A. Walker and C. Walker, eds). London: Child Poverty Action Group.

Conservative Party (1983). *Conservative Party Manifesto 1983.* London: Conservative Central Office.

Conservative Party (1987). *Conservative Party Manifesto 1987.* London: Conservative Central Office.

Conservative Political Centre (1981). *The Future of Marriage.* London: Conservative Central Office.

Craven, E., Rimmer, L. and Wicks, M. (1982). *Family Issues and Public Policy.* London: Study Commission on the Family.

Gittins, D. (1985). *The Family in Question.* London: Macmillan.

Hansard (1986). 13 February, pp. 530–61.

Jenkin, P. (1977). Speech to Conservative Party conference.

Johnson, P. (1982). Family re-union. *The Observer,* 10 October.

Johnson, P. (1987). *Daily Telegraph,* 5 January, p. 12.

Office of Population Censuses and Surveys (1988). *Social Trends.* London: HMSO.

Tebbit, N. (1985). *The Values of Freedom.* London: Conservative Political Centre.

Thatcher, M. (1977). *Let Our Children Grow Tall.* London: Centre for Policy Studies.

7 Health Care

Ray Jobling

The fortieth anniversary of the foundation of the National Health Service (NHS) in Britain fell on 5 July 1988. By common, indeed virtually universal assent, the service represents a major achievement for 'social democratic' government. It is a service valued and cherished by all, even those who choose to insure themselves as individuals so that they may obtain additional or alternative private care. As Conservative politicians rightly point out, it has been Conservative governments who have directed the NHS for most of its history. If it is in 1988 an essential public service organization, still embodying features worth defending in argument and action, then it has to be recognized that its current form and content, with both positive and negative aspects, reflects Conservative policies and administration as much as Labour's. Most commentators would, however, interject that there was a broad political consensus surrounding the NHS until 1979. The coming of 'Thatcherism', however, marked the beginning of a major change in Conservative thinking about the NHS and government health care policy.

[handwritten marginal note: Thatcherism: beginning of a major change towards NHS.]

The first Thatcher Government: 1979–83

The record of the first two Thatcher governments on health policy and the administration of the NHS is already well documented. The 1979 Government did not in fact come into office with notably radical manifesto commitments on health. Despite the political background within the Party which gave emphasis to the need for dramatic, ideologically based change, in relation to the NHS at least, the proposals and promises were modest. Rudolf Klein, reviewing both the manifesto and the actual record of the 1979–83 Government has been prompted to ask whether indeed it represented a 'retreat from ideology' (Klein, 1985:189). The Government placed a clear emphasis upon greater operational efficiency and value for the taxpayer's money. Bureaucracy, with its attendant delays, waste and costs, would be reduced. The private sector would be encouraged to increase individual choice, reduce somewhat the strain on NHS resources, and increase competitive pressure to force efficiency upon the NHS. There was only the vaguest of mentions of a review of the funding or financial basis of the Service. Apparently, the need for caution in dealing with an overwhelmingly popular service prevailed over whatever desire there might have been to transform it for ideological or financial reasons. It is also true that the Party's and Government's advisers had not yet begun to come to grips with the task of finding even superficially plausible alternatives to the well-established NHS principles, provisions and structures. Finally, there was clear recognition of the power of vested interests, not least the medical profession, to resist change and impose electoral damage in the process.

In the event, the first Thatcher Government in practice concentrated upon achieving 'efficiency savings' and obtaining more by way of service from a maintained level of spending. Their efforts complemented and elaborated the moves towards cash limitation inherited from earlier Labour governments. The outcome was of course that the NHS continued to fall behind in the face of rising need and expressed demand, and arguably this process accelerated. Popular discussion focussed more and more upon lengthening waiting times as the evidence of it.

The Government's second priority was to dismantle needless bureaucracy. Reorganization of the Service in 1982 was the major practical manifestation. This was directed towards more local decision making and more precise local accountability. Accordingly, one 'administrative' tier was removed from the structure, with the abolition of Area Health Authorities. But the move towards localization of priority setting and decision making was increasingly contradicted by a tendency towards centralization. Given the major emphasis upon overall cost containment, the Government strengthened the hold of national civil servants. Experience of the difficulties convinced them that local management would have to be made more accountable to the centre. This was to become the focus of the Griffiths Report (1982) which was to be such an important feature of the second Thatcher Government's approach to the NHS.

'Privatization' in its various forms was another key feature of the 1979–83 period. More people began to seek private health insurance cover (partly, probably even largely, in conscious recognition of the increasing strains in the NHS), and the private acute hospital sector began to grow in a significant fashion. More notable, however, was the increased subsidization of the nursing homes sector providing longer-term care for the elderly, via DHSS payments to individuals through the benefits system. This represented an acceleration, if not in a real sense the beginning, of a process which has now transformed the provision of residential care to the rapidly expanding population of very elderly people.

The second Thatcher Government: 1983-7

The 1983-7 Government continued and consolidated the trends established by the first Thatcher administration. This time they came into office without even explicitly indicating a desire (let alone firm intention) to alter the basis of NHS funding. The record shows, however, a strong commitment to cost limitation, efficiency 'savings', stronger 'management', and 'privatization' via contracting out.

Public attention increasingly centred upon disputes surrounding the arrangements and processes of competitive tendering and contracting out ancillary services. It was possible for Ministers to point to financial 'savings'. But it became increasingly hard to deny that standards and quality were suffering. NHS workers (and their replacements working for contractors) had, moreover, paid a high price in reduced earnings and conditions of employment. There were major long-running industrial disputes which attracted widespread sympathy and support for the workers' cause, particularly since their interests and those of the users of the service seemed to coincide. Perhaps more significantly, from the Government's point of view, they damaged attempts to promote a positive public image for the 'privatization' policy.

The Government did, however, have one 'victory', over their attempt to further restrict the rights of General Practitioners (GPs) to prescribe according to their individual professional judgement. In fact, in the end the two sides compromised; but essentially the Government was able to claim that a concession had been won from the doctors, which might well prove valuable in future arguments over other 'principles'.

In the hospitals, however, the strain in budgets began to become more visible and obtrusive. NHS underfunding was to become a political problem of major proportions for the Government. After unemployment, the state of the Health Service was very evidently the most outstandingly weak part of the 'Thatcher' record when the Conservative Party went to the country for the 1987 General Election.

The third Thatcher Government: 1987-

Interestingly, the Conservative Party manifesto for the 1987 election once again promised (or threatened) little that was radical for the NHS. It was to be a case of more of the same. This was despite, or perhaps it was because of, the fact that an air of distinct 'crisis' had come to surround the Service and public perception of it. The newly elected Government responded in part with a 'Let's tough it out' approach. Initially, they blamed poor presentation, a 'bad press' and a ruthless opposition for the poor reputation of their record on the NHS. The argument was that there was no crisis at all. Gradually, however, the political strategy has changed, and the fact of a major, enduring problem over finance has been acknowledged. At the same time it has been asserted that traditional remedies, like yet higher central funding, have demonstrably failed. For the first time since 1979 radical ideas and 'solutions' from the right have begun to surface and attract serious attention. The range of supposed solutions has been wide, however, and much of the advice from the various 'think-tanks' has been contradictory. So sensitive has the review been in the context of some of the suggestions which would in effect transform the Service beyond recognition, that it has had to be held in secret (*The Independent*, 30 January 1989).

The general thrust of policy advice from the radical right is clear, and grounded in relatively simple extensions of the ideas and theories of neoclassical economics. Thus, for example, the virtues of the market and competition are emphasized. For the individual there should be greater choice, and the pursuit of rational self-interest at an individual level will require health care providers to be more efficient as they compete with one another for survival. Individual patients will for their part have to become more aware of the costs of the demands they make upon health services, and be required to bear the consequences of excessive or unrealistic expectations. Much reliance is being placed in these discussions upon experience in other countries, most especially the USA.

Policy advice on health care from the radical right

There has been no dearth of advice from Conservative writers about how the NHS should be reorganized, and more especially financed, in an effort to overcome what they see as the main problem that it represents to the country and economy, viz. public sector *costs*. Ideologically, and for reasons grounded in Conservative economic theory, the Government would prefer not to increase central funding for the NHS. Indeed, they would like to spend *less* taxpayers' money.

Whatever the third Thatcher Government decides to do about the NHS, however, they must start from the realities of the present position. First, there has already been in existence for 40 years, universal tax-financed health care, which is for the most part 'free' at the time of use.

Secondly, opinion polls have repeatedly shown that for all its problems
and faults, the present system is popular and highly valued. The public is
scarcely knowledgeable about alternatives, but is none the less massively
sceptical that radical changes will be beneficial. Thirdly, there is clear
resistance to proposals which would erode fundamental principles and
provision from among those who work in the Service – even those who
are by instinct and habit, 'conservative'. What then is feasible from the
Government's and the Conservative Party's point of view?

Charges

Charges have been levied for specific items of the Service from almost
the very beginning in the NHS. They represent a source of revenue,
albeit up to now some would argue, a minor source in the context of the
total budget. Revenue from charges in fact accounts for no more than 3%
of NHS funding. However, there could be charges for each item, and for a
wider range of items or services. The Adam Smith Institute, for example,
have argued that 'There is a strong case for charging the full cost of
family planning services ... welfare cases would have the fees waived'
(1984:26). They advocated charging for 'non-urgent ambulance journeys'
too, ' ... perhaps at the same rate as prescriptions. For welfare-case credit
card holders, it might be possible to reimburse the cost of their journeys
on public transport at a set rate which would, hopefully, be cheaper than
the average journey cost by ambulance' (loc. cit.). This would generate
more income, but would more importantly encourage cost-consciousness,
and thereby act as a deterrent to 'unreasonable' or 'unnecessary' demand.

The Thatcher governments have repeatedly increased prescription
charges, while at the same time protecting the exemptions to which such
a large proportion of the population are entitled. They have also extended
and increased charges for dental and ophthalmic services, riding out initial
storms of protest. There has been a notable reluctance to go beyond this,
however, even where there have been many years of consideration, e.g.
the introduction of bed and board, 'hotel' charges for hospital in-patients.
The Adam Smith Institute's 1984 estimate of the charge which would be
associated with an 'average' visit to hospital, was in the region of £50.
They said, however, that 'It may, of course, be possible for a hospital to
offer different standards of comfort and to levy different charges
accordingly' (1984:25). A Centre of Policy Studies author suggested in
1986, a 'modest' hotel fee of a minimum of £15 a night and a maximum of
£75 for a stay, urging that this could be 'insured against at little cost'
(Elwell, 1986:7). The fact of the matter is that it would be administratively
costly to raise from this source only a relatively modest sum of money,
and at a potentially high political 'cost'.

To quote two Conservative policy analysts:

the imposition of any charge has always led to the most caustic political arguments. The natural desire of all governments to avoid such storms must seriously limit the prospects of charges for NHS services becoming a major contributor to the overall budget (Butler and Pirie, 1988:14).

They conclude that 'the inevitable hardships that would be caused by a general policy of charges do not help politicians to feel more warmly to the idea' (1988:15). The same sum could be derived from general taxation with considerable ease, and with far less political damage. In any case, the extra revenue might just be used as a substitute for tax moneys, rather than as an addition to the total sum available for health. It would not help to satisfy public pressure for more to be spent on health.

According to the Adam Smith Institute (1984:27), once charges had been introduced for

non-essential ambulance journeys, non-essential drugs; hotel and general services, some GP services, and so on . . . it makes sense to extend the pricing principle more deeply into medical care, and to begin charging for a number of minor medical services.

Elwell (1986:7) also took for granted that all patients, 'other than those receiving family credits should pay a modest fee for visits, and more if they visit a "new" GP. GPs would not, of course, be obliged to accept payments.'

All of this advice notwithstanding, more recently two influential policy advisers counselled against universal charging, saying that certainly it could not by itself constitute an adequate response to the defects of the present system (Letwin and Redwood, 1988:15).

Private health insurance and public/private sector 'mix'

Private insurance has already grown significantly, most notably on the basis of negotiated 'group' enrolments by employers. It has become a key element of employee benefit packages, i.e. a 'perk'. This could be given further encouragement via tax concessions. There could be a real political reward as private insurance became accessible to a wider range of the employed population. 'The more new entrants, of course, the more defenders of private insurance there are in any political arguments about its future' (Butler and Pirie, 1988:19). There is also the argument that 'people might be readier to pay more if the additional funds were to be spent directly on themselves and their families. Additional taxation might meet with less support' (Butler and Pirie, 1988:28).

Much has been written supporting tax incentives for private health insurance premiums. However, they have it seems, a powerful opponent. The Treasury objects that while revenue losses are real, any savings are notional. For this reason, and others, many of the advocates put it forward as no more than a limited way of tempting people into the private sector so as to buy time for the NHS. Thus it is said that pressure would thereby come off public funds, and more brought in from private sources. But others have a vision which is far wider and sharper. Those covered by private insurance would increasingly leave the NHS altogether, providing for significant savings for the State sector. The Adam Smith Institute (1984:30) portrayed this future clearly enough:

> The boost to private health services which this would bring is considerable. Many of those presently working in the state sector would find it congenial to transfer and there would be considerable scope for private sector firms to take over complete NHS installations for their own use, further improving the revenue available to be spent on deserving cases by the state system.

'Thatcherite' writers on health care cannot as yet agree upon whether deliberately and dramatically to remix the NHS and private sector elements of the total health care provision available to the population. Most, however, have seen a continuing role for State hospitals, but in competition with private sector providers, and indeed with one another. Citizens could then choose whichever represented the 'best buy' at any one time in a new health care marketplace. The advantages put forward are greater consumer choice, more flexibility, and more obvious incentive to efficiency. It is far from clear, however, that such a programme relying upon a private insurance strategy would actually increase the total funds available for health care. We would still find ourselves rationing it, in much the same way as now. Some on the political right have taken to talking about health 'credits' or 'vouchers' to guarantee that even those who could not pay for private insurance, or who would be deemed uninsurable 'poor risks', would be able to enter the market for care. These discussions, it is notable, avoid the use of the term 'ration coupons' or 'rationing', though this is indeed what is being contemplated and discussed. Despite this, when they become more precise in their recommendations, for example in making a comparison with the US model of Health Maintenance Organizations (HMOs) or Health Management Units (as in the discussion by Butler and Pirie, 1988), then it becomes clear that the objective is not simply to reduce costs via greater efficiency, but also to restrict 'demand' and ration supply in a money saving effort. Goldsmith and Willetts (1988), in their 'health review' prefer the term and concept 'Managed Health Care Organization' noting that for them the essence of a new system in Britain would have to include the better management of public money, cost control, patient choice and efficient service delivery. They concentrate in 1988, it is interesting to note, upon radical service *reform* of, and not an outright challenge to, the NHS. But in 1984 the Adam Smith Institute (1984:33) discussed HMOs as being:

> most likely to spring up in an atmosphere where private insurance is widespread – and therefore the principles of subscription medicine and private practitioners are common – than from the bedrock of socialized medicine .

There is bound to be an on-going debate in Britain during the period of the third Thatcher Government of the pros and cons of the USA's HMO model, or variants of it. An informed critical assessment of the American experience will be essential even by the right, and its advocates will have to offer reassurances concerning the evidence that poorer people would do worse by way of health outcomes under such a system, than they would under a properly funded and well-managed NHS.

The radical right have begun to redefine and recast their own agenda for changing Britain's health care. They remain convinced, of course, of the virtues of the market and competition (evidenced best perhaps by Peet, 1988) even where it is clear that a 'reform' of the NHS is what is being proposed and not a radical transformation, let alone the dismantling of it. Closer reading may, however, lead critics to the conclusion that a wolf lies hidden beneath this sheep's clothing of nothing more than a little healthy competition. They may too be forgiven if they are amused by Peet's enthusiasm for competition for the NHS from private providers, when simultaneously he urges the 'need for some protection of the private sector if the consumer is to get all the benefits of competition in health-care delivery' (Peet, 1988:31).

An assessment of the state of the NHS in 1988 after roughly a decade of Thatcher governments shows that there have been changes. Most independent observers recognize that the Service has been and is substantially under-financed. Funding has just not kept pace with rising need, stemming from demographic changes in particular. Nor has it taken into account changes in the pattern of care – and not merely because of technological advances, but in terms of the rising costs of a shift towards more expensive community-based care for individuals who would otherwise have been (by comparison) relatively cheaply 'warehoused' in long-term institutional settings. Finally, the Government has systematically, and at times cynically, imposed new burdens upon Health Authorities and yet underfunded them. This has been so when they have 'assumed' efficiency savings, which have been impossible to achieve. It has also been so when they have simply not met in full, pay settlements which have been agreed nationally. They have had to be paid for in effect out of funds which would otherwise have gone to services. Despite this, the continuing circumstance of low pay at a time when more generally those in work have benefited from rising earnings (and more recently reduced taxes on their higher earnings) as well as attractive benefits packages, has impelled many NHS workers to seek employment elsewhere. Many parts of the Service suffer chronic staff shortages, and at times crisis point has been reached and services temporarily discontinued as a result.

The position in 1988

The service is no longer actually available to those who need it at their time of need, irrespective of an ability to pay, and free at that point of time. It has to be conceded that the Thatcher governments may have done little by way of a *radical* departure from pre-1979 principles, policy or practice in charging, providing for private insurance and private medicine, and the like. But they have extended and elaborated such elements of the system. Prescription charges for those who pay them have, for example, been increased substantially. Moreover, they have done little to improve access to care (nor speed of access) for the mass of people who need it. There have been gainers and losers, of course. On the whole, the normally healthy, young, better off, employed in the South-East have been gainers. The losers are predictably the unemployed, claimants, poorly paid, and chronically sick everywhere. These facts reflect the position pre-Thatcher, of course. The evidence is there for all to see in the Black Report on *Inequalities in Health* (1980). But Conservative Health Ministers since its publication have shown no sign of any willingness to depart from the view put forward by the Secretary of State in August, 1980, on receipt of it, when he said that the additional expenditure of £2 billion plus, which the Working Group recommended, 'is quite unrealistic in present or any future foreseeable economic circumstances' (Black Report, 1980: Foreword). In consequence, the publication of the Health Education Council's Report *The Health Divide* (1987), with its confirmation of increasing economic and social polarization with consequential damaging effects on health, came as no surprise. Nor did the negative reactions to the Report from many in government, the premature departure from office of the Council's Director, and the 'reconstruction' of the Council to take the form of a more accountable Special Health Authority, i.e. The Health Education Authority.

The radical right have begun to put forward a variety of proposals for reform of the health care system and the NHS in particular. But the more radical the ideas, the more they have been found wanting, in either practical or just as importantly 'political' terms. Some Conservative writers, it is true, have sought to address the problem of under-financing for health care. Few would argue with their assertion of the need to review the disposition of resources between particular services; nor with their demands for value for money and efficiency. But none has yet shown any commitment at all to a more adequate level of central finance from taxation. This is, of course, directly attributable to their ideological and economic preconceptions which lead them to require tax cuts. They have preferred 'solutions' which limit overall funding and strengthen managerial controls over budgets without seriously attending to the outcomes in terms of the quality and effectiveness of treatment and care. In short, they have failed to demonstrate a concern for *need* which matches their emphasis upon restricting public expenditure, limiting demand and efficiently managing resources.

Many of the supposed 'solutions' put forward reflect a direct and unashamed reliance upon the model of private, profit-orientated business. They deny, in their stress upon service to individual subscribers and consumers, where paying more entitles you to receive more, the more basic of the original values underpinning the NHS – that of collective responsibility for provision to meet the needs of all on an equal basis, according solely to need and medical priority. While the Thatcher governments may have held back from the more radical steps urged by some Conservatives, history may yet prove that their most lasting mark has been to prevent us from introducing much needed measures to reduce inequality in health status.

Beyond Thatcherism: The alternatives

Any discussion of where health policy and the NHS should and will go after Thatcherism must take into account that the third term of office will run until 1991–2. The Conservatives may, given their substantial majority, win again. It is possible that by then 'Thatcherism' will have been replaced by an alternative Conservative 'tendency', but in 1989 there are few who would say this is a probability.

An argument has been advanced here that the more radical suggestions from the right about the NHS and its restructuring have not in fact been adopted by the Thatcher governments. Instead, they have relied upon already tried and tested devices to secure the desired results (however, see *The Independent*, 1989). In particular, the Service has been, despite all of their denials, deprived of the funds essential to keep pace with need. Britain does lag behind most advanced societies in its level of health care spending. They have, too, sought to privatize and individualize the costs of sickness, through charging NHS patients more (and for more), and through their encouragement to private insurance. There have also been significant advances for private sector suppliers of services, and the investor-owned, 'for-profit', health care companies have grown substantially. Their 1988 Review is likely to result in developments of these trends, plus greater efforts to restrict the demand for care. In effect, by the end of the third term, there will be a 'tiered' service to a far more substantial degree than was the case in 1979. At best they have accepted increased inequality of access to health care and its consequences. At worst they have enthusiastically sought it, using it as a device to reward those who in their eyes are 'thrusting' wealth creators, and to threaten or discipline the rest. Health has, after 40 years, been *deliberately* rather than unintentionally taken back into the systematic generation of inequality.

Those advocating alternative approaches to health care must attend to the crisis in funding which affects the NHS. Much more public money will have to be put into the service in the short term to overcome the immediate problems. This is a matter, however, of 'buying time' while longer term policies are implemented. None the less, there can be no serious alternative, short or long term, to funding the service in the main from general taxation. This is the most cost-effective and only fair way of generating the necessary finance for it.

Perhaps the most serious financial problem to be faced, however, is staffing and low pay. The NHS has always relied upon a vast army of poorly paid workers. If they are to be paid a fairer wage, and undeniably they should be, then the cost implications are serious. Money must be diverted from less essential services, and if necessary more revenue must be generated. In the process there will be hard choices to make.

There can be no other basis for priority-setting than national review and national decision making. The Thatcher governments have taught us that it is possible to set and keep to strong national policy and managerial 'guidance'. Within that framework, Health Authorities should be allowed to establish plans for meeting distinctive local problems and needs. But the service will have to retain an emphasis upon sound management while transforming the 'culture' to bring new community-sensitive, genuinely participative decision making. No future government should seek to avoid in the longer term, further structural upheaval, in spite of the pain of previous reorganizations. Separate Health Authorities, Family Practitioner Committees and Social Service Departments of local authorities, make no sense today, if ever they did. Who could deny, too, that simply responding to sickness and individual crisis is a mistake. Public policy and provision should be directed towards improving the standard and quality of life in a way which will make the community 'healthier'. Thus we must again recognize that housing, childcare provision, social services, recreational facilities and the like are part of *health* policy. Encouragement, support and, if necessary, direction, would have to be given to employers too, to pursue policies geared to the welfare of their employees and families.

For the foreseeable future, whatever valuable immediate changes are introduced, it should be obvious that health care in Britain will in effect be 'rationed'. At present, and indeed from virtually the inception of the NHS, this has been achieved by straightforwardly de-advertising, restricting or failure to supply, charging and queueing. While it may be possible to be more socially aware and responsible in the use of these devices, it is unlikely that they will disappear. For this reason the opportunity to bypass the system would have to be contained and regulated in the interests of social equity. The private market for health is in any case price-sensitive, and relatively simple government action could bring, if desired, quick results. Private sector funds and facilities could, however, be used to complement and assist the NHS, through, for example, negotiating advantageous access for public sector patients. In this sense, something could be learned from the Thatcher years.

Overall, however, those planning and providing the service in the future have much to learn from the public in their thinking about the way forward for the NHS. The public are ready for sensible modest reform, which will bring quicker, better care when they need it. Primary care services are widely applauded for the most part. Hospital care is praised, when and once it is obtained. Community services and long-stay care are widely recognized to require urgent attention. Psychiatric services are known to be deprived to a point of scandal. People are prepared to pay through taxes and even modest charges for a good service. They are ready to pay more if there is going to be a better service. But they resent poor quality in the public sector. They regret, too, that private sector care goes to a privileged few, being rightly offended by the unfairness of it.

In summary, broadly speaking, they want the service *as it is*, with only modest reform, to work, and to work well. They are also accepting (when they are asked to think about it) of professional concern to move towards preventative measures and health promotion. In other words, there would be massive public support for an initial programme of limited reform in the context of a more appropriate level of funding. Talk of 'revolutionary' change from the left will dismay the general public just as much as it has when it has come under the Thatcher governments from the radical right. The real alternative to 'Thatcherism' which is plausible and practical is to run the existing service effectively on the basis of the NHS's original sound principles, while simultaneously planning a more integrated structure for delivering basic multidisciplinary, community-based care in the future. Most important of all in political terms, is that there is an overwhelming majority for such a course among professionals and the wider electorate alike.

References

Adam Smith Institute (1984). *Omega Report – Health Policy*. London: Adam Smith Institute.

Black, Sir D. (1980). *Inequalities in Health*. London: HMSO.

Butler, E. and Pirie, M. (1988). *The Health of Nations*. London: Adam Smith Institute.

Elwell, H. (1986). *The NHS: The Road to Recovery*. London: Centre for Policy Studies.

Goldsmith, M. and Willetts, D. (1988). *Managed Health Care: A New System for a Better Health Service*. London: Centre for Policy Studies.

Griffiths, Sir R. (1982). *Report of the NHS Management Inquiry*, London: DHSS.

Health Education Council (1987). *The Health Divide*. London: Health Education Council.

Independent, The, 30 January 1989.

Klein, R. (1985). Health policy 1979–83: The retreat from ideology. In *Implementing Government Policy Initiatives* (P. Jackson, ed.). London: RIPA.

Letwin, O. and Redwood, J. (1988). *Britain's Biggest Enterprise – Ideas for Radical Reform of the NHS*. London: Centre for Policy Studies.

Peet, J. (1988). *Healthy Competition: How to Improve the NHS*. London: Centre for Policy Studies.

8 Social Work

Mike Nellis

This chapter is concerned with the influence of the present Conservative Government on social work. It seeks to set its influence in the context of wider policies towards the personal social services, and to ascertain what the existing literature of radical social work can tell us about a possible way forward.

The New Right and the personal social services

Throughout most of the 1980s, until the beginning of Mrs Thatcher's third term, it has not been quite as easy to identify New Right policies towards the personal social services as it has been towards education and the NHS. Although they have made many general attacks on the Welfare State, the think-tanks such as the Institute of Economic Affairs, the Adam Smith Institute and the Centre for Policy Studies, have rarely made personal social services an explicit target. At first sight, given the way in which the personal social services and in particular the figure of the social worker have become emblematic of the 'dependency culture' which the Thatcher Government and the think-tanks are seeking to eradicate, this may seem odd. There is, however, a simple explanation, namely that the relatively new 'personal social services' created by the Seebohm reorganization in 1971 have never been as high in public esteem as education and the NHS, and have therefore been vulnerable to restructuring by indirect means rather than the frontal assaults that have been deemed necessary to weaken public faith in more traditional institutions.

This sense of indirectness of pressure from the outside, is certainly how leaders of Social Services Departments have perceived their situation during the Thatcher years (Parker, 1987).

That is not to say, however, that there have been no explicit New Right criticisms of social work, or that the Thatcher Government has not in fact had an implicit policy on the personal social services. Morgan's (1978) attack on the therapeutic pretensions of social work with young offenders, and Brewer and Lait's (1980) more wide-ranging critique proved to be straws in the wind, and while their overall tone and perspective were easily rejected by social workers, both contained small elements of truth which were not easily repudiated. Between them they opened up the possibility of further questioning by the right, and Brewer and Lait in particular lent support to the view, prevalent at the time in a variety of circles, that an official enquiry into social work was urgently needed.

Inadvertently, these writers also contributed to the process of doubt that began to assail the left-wing critics of social work (hitherto the 'radicals'), in the wake of the social work strikes of 1978-9. By emphasizing incompetence, pretentiousness and professional self-aggrandizement, Morgan, Brewer and Lait made the left realize that popular sympathy did not lie with a socialist account of social workers as (largely) the 'soft police' of capitalist society. However, to the extent that they too made use of libertarian arguments to challenge what they saw as the intrusive, controlling functions of social work – the lackeys of a 'nanny state' – they stole much of the left's thunder.

The Government has made no single, coherent statement on personal social services. A Green Paper was promised by Secretary of State Norman Fowler in an influential speech at Buxton in 1984, but it never materialized, apparently because of more pressing demands to reform Social Security and the NHS (Hencke 1986). The development of policy in this area has therefore to be pieced together from a variety of different sources, notably the Barclay Report (1982), the Audit Commission (1986) and, most recently, the Griffiths Report (1988), as well as ministerial speeches. These reports were not as trenchant in tone as Brewer and Lait had been, and in so far as they persistently gave a key role to local government – the attack on which, particularly in terms of rate-capping, provided the backcloth to much Conservative policy on social services – they were not always fully consistent with New Right ideology.

Government policy on the personal social services, and the extent of its impact, became clearer with the onset of Thatcher's third term in 1987. Social, as opposed to economic, policy moved to the top of the Government's agenda. The combination, within a few days of each other, of a budget which blatantly favoured the rich and legislation which reduced social security payments to the poor, constituted the most far-reaching changes to the Welfare State since its expansion at the end of the Second World War. Penalizing the poor, weakening State welfare and giving incentives to the rich were the means by which the 'enterprise culture' was to be brought into being.

Looking back from Griffiths to the original 9% cut in social services expenditure which the Conservatives made when they first came to office, it is possible to discern what its overall strategy has been:

> a series of what seemed as they occurred to be separate policy developments may now be seen as part of the Conservative Government's strategy towards the social services. The aim was to turn local authority social services from the main providers of services into something far more limited; the provider of those residual services which no-one else could or would take on (Walker, 1988).

Walker discerns 'three main dimensions' to this process of 'residualization'. First, the deliberate fragmentation of community care through the creation of a plethora of voluntary and private service deliverers, grant aided by a number of different agencies, including the Manpower Services Commission. Secondly, the expansion of the private sector, especially into various spheres of accommodation, particularly in regard to the residential care of the elderly. Ostensibly, local authorities aim to regulate such private provision, but granting the necessary powers and resources has not been high in Government priorities. Thirdly, although the administration of services is being decentralized and diversified, control over resources is undergoing a reverse process of decentralization, in the interests of more efficient financial management and in a way which vitiates the greater consumer choice and control which decentralization implies.

The residualization of the statutory social services (which are notionally universal), and the expansion of the private and voluntary sectors in a geographically *ad hoc* fashion, represents a major change of direction in post-war social policy, back towards selective and inherently stigmatizing services. While there are no guarantees that the non-statutory sectors (often supported by public funds) will be of high quality, it is almost certain that the remaining statutory authorities will be under-resourced and of a poor standard. While erstwhile clients will be the main group to suffer as a result, they will not be the only losers. As Walker (1988) notes:

> There is also the impact on those who provide the services – home helps, residential care workers and social workers are bound to suffer a crisis in morale as they see the services they provide suffering.

It is to the fortunes of social workers under Thatcherism that we now turn.

Social work since Barclay

Social work grew from being a philanthropic activity in the nineteenth century, targeted at the 'deserving poor', to a high-profile local authority service in the late 1960s and early 1970s. The merging of the diverse post-war strands of social work into a unified 'profession' that occurred as a result of the Seebohm Report reflected a coincidence of interests between social work élites and the Labour Party; but as the latter's fortunes altered, and as expenditure cuts began to bite, this alliance broke down:

> During its expansionary period, social work seemed to be constructed on an enormous landmass of consensus; suddenly in 1980 it appeared to be perched on a tidal sandbank. It had been allowed to be built up under governments of both parties largely for reasons of political expediency. Because of the lack of any firm political commitment to such notions as community care, preventive work, decarceration or even family support, all these aspects of social work were vulnerable to the rising right-wing tide (Jordan and Parton, 1983:6–7).

It was in the late 1970s' climate of expenditure cuts and attacks on social workers' competence that the Government established the Barclay Committee to examine the role and tasks of social workers. Although conducted under the auspices of the National Institute of Social Work, its chairman was a banker with no obvious qualifications for the job, and there were immediate fears that setting up the Committee was merely a circuitous way of legitimating a contraction of the profession's activities. In the event, the report, when it appeared in 1982, was an agreeable surprise. It found many positive things to say about existing social work practice and had no fundamental quarrel with its main base in local authorities. It made a sharp distinction between 'social care planning'– the management and co-ordination of services – and the delivery of services themselves, which may or may not be the responsibility of social workers. Through its key concept of 'community social work', it sought a technical rather than a political solution to the increasing scarceness of resources for welfare, although the concept itself was little more than a restatement of a Seebohm ideal which had always had a small band of professional supporters. Community social work was envisaged as a partnership between the statutory, voluntary and, especially in the Barclay version, the informal sectors of care, the latter consisting either of pre-existing networks of neighbourhood and family care, or networks that could be created by the efforts of the social services. It was this element which provided the link to the populism of Thatcherite ideology.

In fact, the idea of community social work attracted support across the entire political spectrum of social work. Initially, however, it was the liberal/left wing of the profession who, in one form or another, most vigorously defended it. Not only was its participatory emphasis ideologically congenial, it also fitted well with the decentralized administrative structures being created by some left-wing councils.

Nevertheless, whether originating from left, right or centre policies, community social work has not been the professional or political panacea that its supporters had hoped for in the early 1980s. Quite apart from the intrinsic difficulties of operationalizing the concept, it has in some respects run counter to other pressures and trends in local authority social services. A more accurate *general* image of social work in Thatcher's Britain is thus provided by an investigation into the management of Brent Social Services Department – an inner-city authority which attempted to 'go patch' – which disturbingly suggested that the disarray found there reflected 'tensions present in social services organisations throughout the country':

> There is a strong desire to make services accessible to the clientele and to develop local resources, those benefits which are thought to flow from patch systems, but at the same time there is a need for policy control, less variation between areas and financial control, all of which imply a degree of centralisation.
>
> There is a wish to treat people holistically, consistent with the generic approach, but also a wish to get the benefits of specialisation, particularly in complex work like child abuse. There is pressure towards community care and the reduction of residential options but also an appreciation of the costs of such a policy and of the 'tidiness' of the residential solution. There is a need for routines to keep the volume of work flowing smoothly but at the same time a recognition of the importance of creativity and entrepreneurship in solving social problems. . . . Decentralisation has brought chaos and impotence rather than locally sensitive service delivery . . . . Genericism and patch in Brent has meant that there is no structural protection for people whose needs do not fall into immediate high risk categories (Challis, 1987:7).

The degree of risk experienced by some of the youngest clients of social workers was repeatedly thrown into sharp relief during the 1980s by the explosion of child protection work and, more particularly, by a series of enquiries into child deaths. The media image of social workers failing to cope with this risk, however atypical of the profession's general, but unlauded, response, lent support to the view promulgated by Brewer and Lait (of social workers as 'incompetent'), and tended to dominate public debate about them. It also contributed to the development of 'defensive social work' (Harris, 1987) in childcare, erring on the side of caution and intervening early – perhaps too early – to avoid public censure if a child is abused or killed. As emergency removals from home and the assumption of parental rights by local authorities increased as a result, this in turn fuelled latent anxieties about social workers as scornful busybodies, discovering problems where none existed and invading the privacy of ordinary families. Social workers came rightly to feel that whatever they did they could not win. The Government has shown a patent lack of interest in this dilemma and has neither sought to give social workers a clearer mandate to intervene, nor the resources to work preventively before crisis point is reached. It seems unlikely that such resources will ever materialize but it remains to be seen whether the child care legislation expected in Autumn 1988, building on the 1986 White Paper and also incorporating the recommendations of the Cleveland child sex abuse enquiry, will clarify the mandate.

There have been few, if any, positive images of social workers in the press or in government statements during the Thatcher years, and the motif of incompetence has on occasion proved inadequate to the task of discrediting them. At its most extreme, in Thatcher's own pronouncements, the official view has come to be that social workers, far from being a solution to any kind of problem, are themselves part of the problem, especially the problem of 'law and order', but also of the 'dependency culture' which is alleged to have sapped individual resourcefulness and enterprise, and undermined a once healthy respect for self-help. In a speech celebrating the onset of her third term, Mrs Thatcher made plain her views of social work's complicity in lawlessness:

> We must ... restore a clear ethic of personal responsibility. We need to establish that the main person to blame for each crime is the criminal himself. But if anyone else is to blame, it is the professional progressives among broadcasters, social workers, and politicians who have created a fog of excuses in which the mugger and the burglar operate (Thatcher, Speech to the Conservative Central Council, 19 March 1988).

It is in the sphere of training that the Thatcher Government has most recently made clear, by default, its attitudes towards professional social work. Training in both social work (CQSW) and social care (CSS) has been loosely co-ordinated by the Central Council for Education and Training in Social Work (CCETSW) since 1971 and largely undertaken in universities, polytechnics and, for CSS, in Colleges of Further Education.

The inadequacies of training, especially for residential workers and in the sphere of child care, has long been recognized and both of Blom-Cooper's enquiries into child abuse recommended improvements. Even while these were taking place, CCETSW was developing a solution based on the idea that the syllabus needed for basic training was too large to be accommodated in 2-year courses. They proposed extending this to 3 years and asked for £40 million to finance the new arrangements. In May 1988 the Government predictably turned this down, offering only £1 million for improvements to existing training.

Support for CCETSW's proposals had never in fact been universal within social work, with cogent criticism coming from both conservative and socialist quarters, the latter in the form of the National Association of Probation Officers' belief that 3 years' training would further encourage an élitist view of social work and deter mature applicants to the profession, in so far as they would be unable to make the financial sacrifices that 3 years required. None the less, most of the social work lobby reacted with outrage and indignation at the Government's repudiation of CCETSW's proposals, and took it as the rebuff to social work that it was presumably intended to be.

Whither radical social work?

The literature of radical social work has tended to be introspective, debating only with itself and with the social democratic traditions of social work. There has been little attempt to engage with the criticisms of the New Right, precisely because they have been so nebulous and indirect, and certainly since Thatcher's 1987 election victory it has been more or less silent, apparently immobilized by confusion and uncertainty. This has centred on two issues, the long-standing one of whether or not radical social work involves a distinct kind of practice, and the somewhat newer one, forced on it by changed political circumstances, of its relationship to socialism under a government hellbent on writing the latter's epitaph.

The view that Social Services Departments ought to espouse a philosphy of equality had never been accepted, not least on grounds of technical feasibility (Webb and Wistow, 1987:51), and the limits on what social workers could achieve politically, either as individuals or as an organized profession, had been thoroughly mapped out by the mid-1970s (Pearson, 1975). Even allowing for this, the biggest difficulty confronting radical left-wing social workers in the mid-1980s is its failure to spell out what it means to practise socialist social work in a political environment where socialism is in extreme crisis, and unable to offer organizational, and possibly even ideological, support to social work.

What the left have failed to acknowledge is the difficulty of conceptualizing an authentically socialist social work at a time when the fundamentals of socialism are themselves being re-evaluated. It is no longer possible to read off socialist or Marxist principles for social work from socialism or Marxism in general, for it is no longer obvious what larger praxis these might involve. That is not to say that there are no firm proposals around, but merely to indicate that there are many competing, and some diametrically opposed, visions of what the socialist project should involve in the late twentieth century. These competing visions are already evident in some areas of social work practice, for example, systems management versus preventive work, but have thus far not emerged as key issues for many of the theorists and tacticians of radical social work.

That is not to say that nothing of practical value has been produced by the radical social work movement: quite the opposite. It has produced a body of work which, as Webb (1981:72) rightly points out, 'commends itself as an inventory of sensitive practice which should be examined by anyone irrespective of overt political loyalties' and a number of articles within the corpus contain profound and insightful ideas for socialists in social work at the present time. While what follows is inevitably a rather personal selection, it seems to me that the early work by Pearson (1974, 1975), Leonard (1975) and Cohen (1975), and later work by Hugman (1980), Lee and Pithers (1980), Jordan and Parton (1983) Britton (1983) and Bowl (1986), and the various contributions on feminism and social work (Wilson, 1980; Hale, 1983) still have much to offer contemporary practitioners. However desirable it may be to let the romantic pretensions of some social work in the 1970s slide into decent obscurity, it does seem important to keep alive the ideas of Brazilian educator Paulo Friere, via Leonard (1975), and the strategies of Norwegian criminologist Thomas Mathiesen, via Cohen (1975). They represent significant developments in twentieth-century socialist thinking, and are potentially transferable to settings outside of those in which they were generated.

At the present time, in Thatcher's Britain, the strand of radical social work influenced by deviancy theory and humanistic psychology – coupled with Mathiesen's 'politics of abolition' – is the only kind of radical social work that stands a chance of being put into practice.

With Hugman (1980) I regard this as adequately commensurate with socialist ideals in the late 1980s: the most that *social work* can presently hope for. It is a form of practice which serves to help clients (as individuals, groups and neighbourhoods), which serves to bolster the morale and commitment of workers, and which symbolically undermines some key tenets of Thatcherism. It does not of itself redress poverty, other than in some individual cases, or inequality. But the desirability of their abolition can and should be proclaimed by social workers who, as information gatherers on the effects of government policy and as citizens, may well contribute to the process, but the main struggle for social change takes place, if at all, outside the occupational arena of social work. To admit this is also to recognize that it is extremely difficult to be 'in and against the State'. To exaggerate the risks of incorporation in the 1980s, comes dangerously close to the shooting-oneself-in-the-foot escapades of some radical social work in the 1970s, in which social workers and social work academics routinely castigated themselves for being either manipulative, repressive or ineffective, only to find, after 1979 that they had played unwittingly into the hands of the New Right, who had arrived at quite similar judgements from a different intellectual route.

We should perhaps note that Brewer and Lait (1980:111) always took the humanistic version of radical social work seriously enough to suggest that its influence in local authorities be curtailed, on the grounds that 'the use of public position to pursue political objectives under the cover of alleged professional competence' was 'contemptible'. Certainly Mrs Thatcher's denigration of social workers in her Buxton speech as 'professional progressives' who provide alibis for criminals suggests that there is still an element of ideological threat to Thatcherism in what they do, around which she is still seeking, not altogether successfully, to mobilize popular support. Were it not for the fact that in much social work with offenders, for example, there is now an eminently Tory emphasis on personal responsibility (which, *in extremis*, would probably elicit Thatcher's admiration), social workers could take pride in the threat which the Government's image of them (in its more charitable moments) as misguided *altruists* appears to represent.

The way forward

I believe that there is a way forward for socialist social work in Britain, both in terms of practical face-to-face work and in terms of a wider political strategy. The latter depends on precisely the kind of rediscovery that I referred to earlier, in so far as it makes use of Thomas Mathiesen's neglected notion of 'the politics of abolition', a strategy first adapted for social work by Cohen (1975) but still not widely known, or even understood, and still not made use of even in the penal context in which it was first developed (Bottoms, 1987).

First, however, I would like to address the context of social work as it is likely to be practised in the 1990s. I am assuming for the time being that SSDs and SWDs will remain in existence, albeit with a greater emphasis on co-ordination rather than on service delivery, although discussion of alternative structures has taken place (Rea Price, 1987). It has become one of the axioms of good social work literature, and of practice, that poverty exacerbates the problems with which social workers routinely deal. The increase in absolute poverty occasioned by the Social Security reforms in April 1988, and the increase in relative deprivation after the 'tax-cuts-for-the-rich' budget a few weeks earlier, augurs badly for the future of social work. It will simply become more difficult to help people whose basic difficulty is lack of money and perhaps more dangerous for social workers who, as representatives of the 'haves', may find themselves more subject to violence and aggression from an increasingly marginalized and disenfranchised population. It is in these terms that Small (1987) has already accounted for the increased incidence of violence towards social workers.

Oppression can brutalize, and it is pointless being sentimental about the quality of life among the new poor. There will be a need to work with and alongside the disenfranchised, as well as through political channels (those remaining) for their enfranchisement. Class analysis remains important, although, as Hearn suggests, it is perhaps secondary to questions around social and biological reproduction:

> Social work is predominantly concerned with patching up or not patching up problems around sexuality, childbearing, marriage, personal identity, illness, handicap, old age, death and bereavement, particularly as they occur in relation to 'family life' (Hearn, 1982:30).

Given that social work 'is done mainly by women and managed dominantly by men" (Hearn (1982:20) saw as the corollary of this that 'feminism [rather than Marxism] is likely to be a more satisfactory basis for any form of radical social work', and since he wrote this there has been some indication of a movement away from Marxism, if not towards a coherently expressed feminism. Bowl (1986), for example, writes of:

> an emergent progressive literature now wrestling free of an orthodox Marxist view that social work is simply a softer controlling wing of an oppressive state...and that the only legitimate, progressive activity for social workers is as members of their trade union.

Feminism, however, has contributed significantly to the recent unearthing of an issue which is currently of great concern to social work, and which has made social workers (and other related welfare professionals) the object of renewed media attention – the issue of child sexual abuse. While social workers have for more than a decade (since the death of Maria Colwell in 1973) run the risk of public condemnation if they fail to intervene to save an abused child's life, but also if they intervene too precipitously and infringe 'parents' rights', one of the most significant aspects of the child sexual abuse 'scandal' which surfaced in Cleveland, is the resistance of the public (as mediated by the press) to accepting the scale, severity and perhaps even existence of the problem. In a veritable orgy of messenger shooting, the social workers and paediatricians who raised the alarm have been roundly condemned for overzealousness. One of the background reasons for this appears to be the extent that child sexual abuse exposes the brutal effects of patriarchy, and rather than face the implications of this, the 'bad news' is simply repressed.

The sceptical public reaction to child sexual abuse may well come to be seen as emblematic of public reaction generally to the problems which social workers seek – for both professional and political reasons – to draw to their attention. Unless the problems of the poor, not just their poverty, but the consequences of brutalization and constraint, can by ideological sleight of hand be reduced to individual failings, they tend to be seen as signs of injustice, creating instability and threatening the security of the wealthy and powerful. The traditional approach of socialist social workers, that of arguing in terms of links between biography, culture and social structure, between private troubles and public or political issues, will be invalidated. It will be replaced either by an ideology of individual pathology, or suppressed altogether, forcing marginalized people to become, in Friere's terms, 'a culture of silence', unrepresented (except perhaps by churches prepared to denounce the personal effects of injustice) in mainstream society.

The sheer difficulty of helping people enmeshed in poverty, the conflicting demands of society (to protect children, but not to infringe 'parental rights'), the discrepancy between the ideals of the job held out by training and the reality of work in under-resourced offices, has already led to high rates of staff turnover, especially in London, and may lead to social workers leaving the profession. Many aspects of statutory social work may become impossible and unattractive (however well remunerated) and, while certain fields of work, e.g. adoption and psychiatric social work, may retain status by virtue of links with established voluntary sector organizations and hospitals, the status of community social workers in inner cities, and in field, day and residential settings is likely to diminish, in turn reducing its attractiveness as a professional career.

For those choosing to remain in work among the disenfranchised, a revaluation of 'professionalism' may occur. This is something which radical social work has always encouraged:

One of the profession's major tasks is to undo the corrupting effects of professionalisation over the last few years. We must cease to mystify ourselves and others with pseudoscientific jargon; put behind us the absurd delusion of 'objectivity'; reject positivism and embrace uncertainty; open our practices and procedures to scrutiny; resist bureaucratisation and the intrusion of illegitimate notions of management and control, and see 'profession' as a means, not an end, and a means which may, one day, or in some circumstances, be redundant. The true interests of [social workers], as relatively low-grade state employees, rest not in foisting upon society notions of their esoteric skills and superior professionalism, but rather in the common struggle for a fair living wage for all, a just and equitable society, and the effective redistribution of wealth and power (Hugman 1980:152–3).

The abandonment of élitism may lead to a reassertion of vocationalism in social work, akin to the vocationalism of worker-priests and indeed of some existing social workers. As Hugman (1980:130) again notes, radical social work requires 'a congruent style of life':

Radical practice grows inevitably out of a thorough, coherent, tough-minded radical stance as a person: it is not something which can be adopted by or attached to a personality which is essentially wedded to orthodoxy and the status quo. In or out of the job the radical personality will not be pushed around by officials; will not remain silent or inactive when s/he is aggrieved; will be aware and unafraid of his/her needs, drives, strengths, weaknesses; will not be afraid of change; will be thoroughly conversant with the political nature of most taken-for-granted habits and behaviour.

If a new breed of vocationally inclined social workers does emerge – and there are already some, but I am speculating hopefully that they will grow in numbers and strength – they could do worse than look to the example of Bob Holman. Holman, a committed Christian Socialist in the tradition of R.H. Tawney, was a former child care officer who subsequently achieved a professorship of social work, only to abandon it to become a community social worker on a council estate in Bath (for 10 years), and subsequently in the slums of Glasgow. Even Brewer and Lait (1980:208) find Holman an attractive figure, but the political perspective from which they implicitly write can lay no claim to his kind of commitment to the poor.

Humanitarianism is an elusive and easily corrupted quality, but the ideal of personalized care for the more neglected and distressed of one's fellow human beings remains both intelligible and defensible in contemporary Britain. Social work, whether of the tending or empowering kind, *is* an expression of humanitarian concern which has not yet lost its identity, nor become fully incorporated into the purely controlling functions of the State. It still seeks to 'care for strangers' (see Ignatieff, 1984). Caring, however, is a distinctly unfashionable virtue in Thatcher's Britain, and it is this perhaps which is the most insidious effect of New Right thinking on social work – and society; it has gone beyond a denigration of socialism and social democracy in their own right, and denigrated a whole matrix of welfare-related concepts (altruism, compassion, concern, decency, caring) which are part of the cement which make civilized society possible. But, as Mrs. Thatcher has said, there is no such thing as society, 'just individuals and families'. Altruism extends no further than to one's nearest and dearest – if it extends that far!

It is the value of prosaic caring which socialist social work must promote alongside its traditional concern with equality and liberty; it must become the vehicle of a broad humanitarianism which promotes the idea of citizenship – central to the left's attempt to reconstruct itself as a coherent opposition (*New Statesman and Society*, 10 June 1988) – in both its collective and individual aspects. Collective in the sense that citizens are equal with each other; no group is marginalized. Individual in the sense that citizens are as fully developed as human beings, and as responsible as it is possible for them to be.

How is this to be promoted, i.e. what form should political action by social workers take? However the vocationally inclined social workers organize themselves, they will need to retain (or build) their links with powerholders on the left, however fragmented, draw support, contribute ideas and provide evidence of the deleterious effects of Thatcher's social and economic policies. In so far as citizenship is becoming an important motif on the left, it is important for social work to generate its own praxis from this concept, apart from the initiatives in 'community social work'. It may be that they will come to be involved in non-violent direct action, more so than at present, on behalf of their client groups as a way of drawing attention to cuts in resources, e.g. vigils outside DHSS local offices, or in regard to local demands for particular services. It seems unlikely that strike action will be used, as the lessons of earlier strikes have generally been that, whatever good they may do for social workers' political consciousness, and to a lesser extent salaries, they are rarely of direct benefit to clients. For social workers to be seen to be acting in any way that could be construed as *self*-interested in the present climate would be an act of political suicide, easily branded as hypocrisy, easily used as a ground for cuts, and ultimately to the detriment of poor people. The decline of interest in striking as an appropriate political tactic for social workers reflects the doubts among them as to the viability of trade unionism as a means of advancing social work interests, both professional and ideological.

'Ideological' is used here in the widest sense to mean the values which social work seeks to promote, its assumptions about society as it is now, and as it might be, rather than just the self-serving ideologies of which no profession or occupational group is entirely free. As Hearn (1982) states, values in social work tend to be discussed in sublime isolation, and regarded as an ideal to which practice must seek to approximate itself, regardless of time or place. This is not the place to embark on a detailed analysis of values, except to say that social work values as traditionally conceived, however genuinely valuable for framing interactions with *individuals*, reflected the one-sided individualism which developed as part of *laissez-faire* ideology in the nineteenth century. It was a concept of individualism that left little room for notions of civic responsibility, communal solidarity, or citizen participation – the ingredients of what socialists once called fraternity. It is around this notion – not too distinct from citizenship itself, and close to the notion of 'sisterhood', about which socialist feminists have remained able to speak without embarrassment – that radical social workers might take political action. But how?

Without a major revaluation of trade unionism in social work there is little indication that this will be an effective avenue. BASW, beset by perennial criticisms of élitism, was only an effective campaigning group on some issues even in social work's heyday, and focusses more on parliamentary lobbying than on the wider public, or the media. Among Probation Officers, NAPO has fared much better than BASW in terms of its joint role as trade union, professional association and penal pressure group, suggesting that a narrower interest base is preferable to the wide range of activities with which BASW and NALGO are inevitably concerned. Within juvenile justice, the Association for Juvenile Justice has shown a political adroitness hitherto lacking in this field of social work. There is, in fact, no shortage of avenues through which campaigns can be conducted, in isolation or through alliances; the voluntary child care organizations, such as Barnardos and National Children's Home, are developing in this area, but how overtly political they can afford, or will choose, to be remains uncertain.

It is here that Mathiesen's (1974) strategy of 'the unfinished' becomes important; it is essentially a way of working for change within a given system or social structure, but without becoming incorporated within it or selling out the interests of those whom you wish to serve, by neglecting humanitarian work. As Cohen (1975:93) notes:

> To avoid working for short-term goals is politically impossible and paralyses action, but reform alone will corrupt long-term work; to work within the system is to risk legitimating it, but to stay out would be wrong.

This seems to capture the dilemma many radical social workers experience. Cohen (1975:92) goes on to argue that 'the unfinished is a programme based on what does not yet exist', a programme which keeps larger goals in mind and chooses carefully – as carefully as possible without benefit of hindsight – between *positive reforms* which would only support and sustain an oppressive structure, and *negative reforms* which would appear to undermine it, and help clients (for which read 'poor people') at the same time. This resistance to positive reforms, to tinkering with systems in order to strengthen them, goes against the conventional strategy of promoting specific alternatives and openly discussing blueprints for change:

> When the establishment demands 'alternatives' before contemplating any changes, they know in advance that they can already lay down the framework for the discussion. The conservative aims remain taken for granted . . . and only the means are debated. The demand for alternatives, then, has a conserving effect. Real opposition-values because of their nature must be long-term and uncertain. So when the opponent is presented with the choice of specifying alternatives he finds it difficult to avoid coming close to the prevailing order in what he suggests (reform) or emphasising completely different values and thereby being defined away as irresponsible or unrealistic. The answer is to always go for abolition and actually to resist the pressure to make positive reforms (Cohen, 1975:94).

Cohen (1975:92) summarizes thus:

> Only an authoritarian political programme cannot tolerate this ambiguity and is constantly looking . . . for clarity about 'the way ahead'. The point is to remain open and capable of growth, to see some ambiguities as irrelevant, never to let oneself be placed.

At one level, Mathiesen's ideas represent a new contribution to socialist theory, a new way of initiating and organizing change from below, a new strategy for the dispossessed. Their novelty as well as their complexity may account for its failure to have had much impact on radical politics. One of the paradoxes of Mathiesen's work – a strategy to avoid incorporation by the powerful – is that it has not yet been incorporated by the powerless.

Social workers are both powerless in 'professional' terms (relative to the authoritarian State of which they are part) and are also among the self-appointed representatives of some of the most powerless people in society. Contrary to the naive critique of the left in the 1970s, they have not always, or even often, shied away from their responsibilities as representatives of the poor, but it would be unwise to exaggerate the influence they had even within a social democratic framework. Notwithstanding recent attempts to make them more coercive and interventionist, i.e. to incorporate them, the status of social workers has declined considerably during the years of the Thatcher Government; as workers *with* the poor they have come to share the stigma *of* the poor. It would be unrealistic, therefore, to expect them, or for them to expect themselves, to have a major influence on political decision makers. They are weak, and they have only the tactics and strategies of the weak available to them, but, given the social goals of the New Right, it is only from a position of weakness that an uncorrupted defence of concern for the dispossessed could be made, and stand a chance of being taken seriously.

References

Audit Commission (1986). *Making a Reality of Community Care.* London: HMSO.

Barclay Report (1982). *Social Workers: Their Role and Tasks.* London: Bedford Square Press.

Bottoms, A. (1987). Limiting prison use: The example of England and Wales. *The Howard Journal*, August.

Bowl, R. (1986). Social work with old people. In *Ageing and Social Policy: A Critical Assessment* (A. Walker and C. Phillipson, eds). Aldershot: Gower.

Brewer, C. and Lait, J. (1980). *Can Social Work Survive?* London: Temple Smith.

Britton, B. (1983). The politics of the possible. In *The Political Dimensions of Social Work* (B. Jordan and N. Parton, eds). Oxford: Blackwell.

Challis, L. (1987). Brent review: Proposals offer prospect of a radical solution to problems. *Social Work Today*, 14 September.

Cohen, S, (1975). It's alright for you to talk; Political and sociological manifestos for social work action. In *Radical Social Work* (R. Bailey and M. Brake, eds). London: Edward Arnold.

Griffiths Report (1988). *Agenda for Action.* London: HMSO.

Hale, J. (1983). Feminism and social work practice. In *The Political Dimensions of Social Work* (B. Jordan and N. Parton, eds). Oxford: Blackwell.

Harris, N. (1987). Defensive social work. *British Journal of Social Work*, **17**, 1.

Hearn, J. (1982). Radical social work – contradictions, limitations and political possibilities. *Critical Social Policy*, **2**, Summer.

Hencke, D. (1986). Whatever happened to the Tory pledge? *Social Work Today*, 8 September.

Hugman, B. (1980). Radical practice in probation. In *Radical Social Work and Practice* (M. Brake and R. Bailey, eds). London: Edward Arnold.

Ignatieff, M. (1984). *The Needs of Strangers.* London: Chatto.

Jones, H. (ed.) (1974). *Towards a New Social Work.* London: Routledge and Kegan Paul.

Jordan, B. and Parton, N. (eds) (1983). Introduction. In *The Political Dimensions of Social Work.* Oxford: Blackwell.

Lee, P. and Pithers, D. (1980). Radical residential child care: Trojan horse or non-runner. In *Radical Social Work and Practice* (M. Brake and R. Bailey, eds). London: Edward Arnold.

Leonard, P. (1975). Towards a paradigm for radical practice. In *Radical Social Work* (R. Bailey and M. Brake, eds). London: Edward Arnold.

Mathiesen, T. (1974). *The Politics of Abolition*. London: Martin Robertson.

Morgan, P. (1978). *Delinquent Fantasies*. London: Edward Arnold.

Parker, A. (1987) Introduction. In *The Future Role of Social Services Departments* (Policy Studies Institute). London: Policy Studies Institute.

Pearson, G. (1974). The politics of uncertainty. A study in the socialisation of the social worker. In *Towards a New Social Work* (H. Jones, ed.). London: Routledge and Kegan Paul.

Pearson, G. (1975). Making social workers: Bad promises and good omens. In *Radical Social Work* (R. Bailey and M. Brake, eds). London: Edward Arnold.

Rea Price, J. (1987). Providing the social services: The options explored. In *The Future of Social Services Departments* (Policy Studies Institute). London: Policy Studies Institute.

Small, N. (1987). Putting violence towards social workers into context. *Critical Social Policy*, **19**, Summer.

Walker, A. (1988). Tendering care. *New Society*, 22 January.

Webb, A. and Wistow, G. (1987). *Social Work, Social Care and Social Planning: The Personal Social Services since Seebohm*. London: Longman.

Webb, D. (1981). Review of Brake and Bailey (eds) Radical Social Work and Practice. *Issues in Social Work Education*, **1**, Summer.

Wilson, E. (1980). Feminism and social work. In *Radical Social Work and Practice* (M. Brake and R. Bailey, eds). London: Edward Arnold.

9 Housing

Sarah Monk and Mark Kleinman

Introduction

In the General Elections of 1979 and 1983, as in those of 1945 and 1964, housing was an important factor in the success of the winning party. However, unlike those earlier elections, the housing issue did not work to the benefit of the Labour vote, but to that of the Conservatives. The Conservatives projected a powerful image of a property-owning democracy and the release of council tenants from 'municipal serfdom' through the creation of a 'right to buy'. Labour's response, by contrast, often appeared defensive and contradictory, without a coherent and positive alternative. In this chapter we look at why and how the right seized the high ground in the housing debate in the late 1970s and 1980s, and outline the task facing the left in trying to win support for an alternative vision.

New Right ideology on housing

As far as housing is concerned, there is a distinction between the first two terms of the Thatcher Government, and the period after 1987. The 1979–87 period incorporated a pragmatic ideology based around the achievement of specific policy goals, such as reducing public expenditure on housing, and encouraging growth in home ownership. In Thatcher's third term, by contrast, there is evidence of a more thorough-going ideological approach which embraces both the owner-occupied and the rental sectors.

The ideology of the New Right, with its emphasis on individual freedom and consumer choice was expressed in housing policy in two main ways. First, home ownership was encouraged and supported and, secondly, spending on council housing was reduced. New investment was to come primarily from the private sector. The growth of council housing was to be halted and even reversed, and its future role was to be mainly that of a welfare tenure, providing a safety net for the very poor. Public expenditure on housing, as well as being reduced in overall terms, was to be shifted from general needs to special needs and from new construction to repair and renewal of the existing stock.

The economic rationale for the switch from State provision to private provision was a belief that free markets are more efficient than central planning. The operation of the price mechanism bringing together demand and supply in the housing market will lead to greater total social benefits than the administrative allocation of housing.

Home ownership was promoted for other reasons as well. Michael Heseltine (1980), Secretary of State for the Environment, said in Parliament:

> There is in this country a deeply ingrained desire for home ownership. The Government believe that this spirit should be fostered. It reflects the wishes of the people, ensures the wide spread of wealth through society, encourages a personal desire to improve and modernise one's home, enables people to accrue wealth for their children and stimulates the attitudes of independence and self reliance that are the bedrock of a free society.

The extension of owner-occupation was seen as a crucial element in the making of a property-owning democracy. Mass home ownership (and, later, mass share ownership) would help to legitimize the more general notion of the private ownership of property.

Cuts in public expenditure on housing were an inevitable consequence of Thatcher's macroeconomic strategy which, particularly in the early period, emphasized the necessity of controlling the Public Sector Borrowing Requirement (PSBR) as part of the fight against inflation (Heald, 1983). Given the difficulty of reducing central government expenditures, much of the burden necessarily fell on local authority expenditure. Furthermore, capital spending is intrinsically less difficult to cut than current spending: for example, it is easier to cancel a planned school extension than to lay off 20% of the teaching staff. The major item of capital spending by local authorities in England and Wales was housing (Hepworth, 1984:34).

Hence, several different strands in the ideology – a belief in the superiority of the market rather than the plan, a wish to legitimize the notion of private property in general, and a macroeconomic policy aim of reducing public expenditure – led to the same conclusion. No more new council houses were to be built, except to meet the special needs of particular groups such as the elderly; and as much as possible of the existing council stock should be transferred into private ownership.

After Thatcher's third election victory in 1987, a more comprehensive housing ideology emerged with the publication of a White Paper (*Housing: The Government's Proposals*, Cmnd 214) which reflected both the importance being given to housing in the third term, and the more developed nature of the Government's thinking on housing. This appeared to follow in part from the eventual acceptance of the fact that there is an upper limit to the spread of owner-occupation among the population: probably at least 25–30% of households will be tenants at any one time.

In the White Paper, the Government set out four main objectives for its future housing policy. The first objective remained to continue the expansion of home ownership, meaning, among other things, the retention of tax relief on mortgage interest. The second objective was to 'put new life into the independent rented sector', with the term 'independent' covering both private landlords and housing associations. Thirdly, the role of local authorities was to be altered, away from direct provision and towards the encouragement of other forms of tenure. Councils were encouraged to see themselves as 'enablers' (definitely the vogue housing word of 1987) 'who ensure that everyone in their area is adequately housed, but not necessarily by them'. Finally, the Government intended to 'focus the use of scarce public money more effectively', by developing a new 'businesslike' financial framework for local authorities and by setting up Housing Action Trusts (HATs) to lever private sector money into areas of public housing.

This Thatcherite critique of the role of the public sector in housing contains two strands – one economic, the other sociological. The first line of attack rests on a neoclassical economic view about *efficiency*. In a market system, the price mechanism ensures that producers respond to market signals and hence ultimately to consumer preferences. In a non-market system, consumer choice is met by administrative, or bureaucratic procedures. While in principle these can be based on the disinterested attainment of social or welfare goals, in practice public sector management tends to respond to the interests of producers (council members, trade unions, bureaucrats) rather than consumers. Public sector management, unlike the private sector, is not subject to the discipline of the market, with its ultimate sanction that inefficiency will eventually lead to bankruptcy. Therefore, breaking up public sector monopolies, introducing private sector competition and making public housing authorities more like the private sector, will be more efficient and more responsive to consumer choice.

The second strand in the argument is very different. The dry abstract world of economic theory is left behind. Public housing is seen as symptomatic of a wider malaise of dependence on the Welfare State, a weakening of the moral fibre of the working class. William Waldegrave, the Housing Minister, has referred to the difficulties of getting people off the 'drug of dependence', and the White Paper refers to 'whole communities [which] have slipped into a permanent dependence on the welfare system from which it is extremely difficult for people to escape'.

Flaws and inconsistencies: the ideology

Over the period 1979–87 Conservative philosophy on housing has developed from basic pragmatism with an ideological flavouring towards a more fully-fledged and comprehensive ideological position. On further examination, however, the ideology is seen to be riven by major inconsistencies and contradictions.

Chief among these is, of course, continued State support for owner-occupation. The doctrine of 'rolling back the State' and government subsidies is a curiously tenure-bound one. Throughout the period of the Thatcher Government, the value of the subsidy given to home owners through their favourable tax treatment, whether it is measured in terms of Mortgage Interest Relief (MIR) or in terms of the lack of taxes on the imputed rental income of a home and the capital gains on sale, has increased steadily. For example, the value of MIR rose from under £1.5 billion in 1979–80 to over £4 billion in 1985–6 (Holmans, 1987; Malpass and Murie, 1987). While the calculation of the relative benefits to tenants and owners of different forms of housing subsidy is a notoriously complex and controversial area, there is general agreement that in the 1980s, the balance of financial advantage has swung decisively in favour of home owners (Ermisch, 1984; National Federation of Housing Associations, 1985). Contrary to the popular myth, it is tenants who subsidize owner-occupiers rather than the other way round.

Furthermore, it is not only through the tax system that the State supports owner-occupation. The 'right to buy' introduced by the Tories in the 1980 Housing Act gave tenants a discount on the market value of their property of between 33 and 50% (later raised to a maximum of 60% for houses and 75% for flats; Forrest and Murie, 1988). This represents an additional capital subsidy to owner-occupation, which has been estimated at £2.9 billion for the period between October 1980 and September 1983 (Malpass and Murie, 1987: 112). Similarly, Government initiatives such as 'Estate Action' and the Housing Action Trusts proposed in the 1988 Housing Bill reflect a recognition that in some areas the transfer of council properties into owner-occupation cannot proceed without the intervention and support of central government.

On a more theoretical level, there are problems with the view of housing as a purely private good. That is, it is implicit in the New Right outlook that the benefits of housing go solely to the individual occupier. If that is the case, then there is no reason why housing should not be allocated in exactly the same way as most other goods and services, i.e. via the price mechanism. But if the good in question is not a purely private good then this model of the housing market breaks down. Space does not permit a full exposition of the way in which housing departs from the ideal assumptions of the standard neoclassical model (for a more detailed discussion, see Le Grand and Robinson, 1984). Here we will simply refer to three types of market imperfection: supply inelasticities, externalities and the 'merit good' argument.

By supply inelasticities, we mean that the supply of housing does not respond flexibly and quickly to changes in demand. These supply inelasticities arise for a variety of reasons: the fixed location of houses (supplies of houses in one area cannot be used to remedy a deficit in another area); the shortage of land suitable or zoned for housing; and the low productivity of the house-building industry. As a result, it is likely that increases in demand will lead not to increased supply, but simply to higher prices.

Secondly, there are *externalities* associated with housing. That is, bad housing imposes costs on others in the community and good housing confers benefits. For example, dry rot can spread from one terraced property to the next, while more generally the value of a property will be affected by the condition and state of repair of others in the street. Such spillover effects include fire risks and the spread of disease. Hence housing cannot be seen purely as a private good with costs and benefits falling solely on the immediate occupier.

Thirdly, housing is an example of a 'merit good' (Musgrave, 1959). Merit goods are those whose social valuation is higher than the individual values expressed by consumers. Individuals on their own may not choose the collectively appropriate level of say health care or education, or housing. Moreover, because of their importance to the general welfare, the State may wish to exercise some sort of direct control over quality and price. In addition, consumers can sometimes be badly informed or misinformed about the costs and benefits of commodities, e.g. tobacco. For all these reasons, there is an argument in favour of some degree of paternalism, overriding individual preferences (Heald, 1983).

If housing is not a purely private good traded in a perfectly competitive market, then the theoretical underpinning of the New Right ideology is seriously weakened. In addition, there are inconsistencies in some of the details of the ideology. First, at least up until 1987, the New Right had no clear view of the proper role of rented housing, whether private or public. In the public sector, as Malpass has pointed out, the Conservatives had a policy on *subsidies* but not on *rents*. That is, Exchequer subsidies to council housing were phased out, but there was no view taken as to what the average level of rents should be (apart from that they should be 'higher'), or how rents should vary between properties and between geographical areas (Malpass, 1988).

Furthermore, many of the accounting conventions used by the Treasury in its definition of public expenditure seem illogical if not absurd. For example, both borrowing by local authorities and the current year's repayments count as public expenditure. If the same conventions held in the owner-occupied sector, a home owner who took out a £50,000 mortgage and made repayments of capital and interest in the first year amounting to £5000 would be deemed to have a total expenditure of £55,000. The Inquiry into British Housing, chaired by the Duke of Edinburgh, pointed out that repayments of capital by local authorities should be netted off their capital spending in order to derive a figure for net capital expenditure. The Inquiry calculated that an extra £455 million would have been available for capital expenditure on housing in 1984–5 with no impact on net capital expenditure or the Public Sector Borrowing Requirement (PSBR), if accounting conventions were changed (National Federation of Housing Associations, 1985:15).

The New Right's concern with the debilitating effects of dependence is also contradictory. Apparently, paying housing benefit to working families on below average incomes or occupational pensioners is likely to sap the moral fibre of the nation, while the provision of mortgage interest relief (at source, so that the tiresome necessities of form-filling are avoided) promotes a healthy yeoman independence. More generally, tax breaks which benefit the middle and upper classes, such as company cars and pension schemes, are not made the object of a morality campaign, and aspects of the Welfare State which benefit predominantly middle-class households, such as student grants, have proved to be less vulnerable to attack from New Right ideologies than those where the majority of recipients and employees are working class (Le Grand and Winter, 1987).

Viewed as a logical, if somewhat ruthless, application of strict economic and moral principles to the provision of housing, both the ideology and the practice of the Thatcher governments seem inconsistent and arbitrary. Indeed, the most plausible thread running through New Right housing ideology and policy is the more secular and pragmatic one of *centralization* – the reduction of the role of local authorities and a corresponding increase in the powers of central government.

The consequences of Thatcherite housing policies

It is usually claimed that one of the great successes of Thatcherism has been a substantial increase in home ownership. Between 1979 and 1987 the number of owner-occupiers in Great Britain increased from

11,520,000 to 14,259,000 or, as a percentage of all households, from 55 to 64%. That is, the number of owner-occupiers rose by 19% over an 8-year period, or approximately 2.4% per year. However, the rate of increase of owner-occupation was little different under the previous Labour administration. Between 1974 and 1979, the number of owner-occupiers increased by 10.2% or approximately 1.8% per year.

Hence, all the *extra* subsidies going to owner-occupation, such as the rise in the MIR ceiling and the massive discounts under the 'right to buy', did not produce any real change in the rate of increase of the owner-occupied sector. What was different about the Thatcher years was that for the first time, the increase in owner-occupation came at the expense of the public sector. Previously, both owner-occupation *and* public housing have been growing, while the private rented sector has declined. This shift has meant that the public sector has moved closer towards a 'residual' role, catering only for the poorest and most disadvantaged households (Malpass, 1983; Clapham and English, 1987).

One major consequence of the policies outlined above has been the rapid fall in new construction in the public sector. Public sector housing starts in Great Britain fell from 107,000 in 1978 to only 30,000 in 1987. There has been a rise in the number of private sector starts, after a trough in 1980, but even so, the total for 1987, at 194,000, was lower than in 1973. The increase in private starts has not been enough to offset public sector decline, so that total starts in 1987 were more than 30% lower than in 1976 (*BSA Bulletin*, January 1988). In addition, there have been important regional differences too, with a marked shift in housing construction from the North to the South (Kleinman and Whitehead, 1988).

The combination of a collapse in new building and the success of the 'right to buy' policy, with around 1 million sales in the UK since 1979, has resulted in longer council waiting lists and a rapid rise in homelessness. Over the last decade, the number of homeless families has doubled to more than 100,000 (Shelter, 1987). In addition, it has been estimated that more than 200,000 households are in 'non-tenure' accommodation on the fringe of homelessness, such as squatting, shortlife, 'bed and breakfast', hostels and sleeping rough (Whitehead and Kleinman, 1986). Moreover, at the same time as the *supply* of council housing has been declining, there has been an increase in the range of households in housing need. Demographic changes have led to increases in the numbers of the elderly and of single-parent families; the policy of 'care in the community' has meant increased demand from those with special needs such as the mentally and physically handicapped; and the continuing decline of the private rented sector has meant that larger numbers of single people and childless couples now seek public housing.

The strain experienced by the public sector in trying to cope with the volume and range of housing needs placed upon it shows graphically in the numbers of homeless households placed in bed and breakfast and other forms of temporary accommodation because no permanent accommodation is available. In March 1987, these amounted to 22,000 families (Central Statistical Office, 1988). The rise in the numbers of families housed in bed and breakfast provides a potent symbol of the underside of privatization in housing. It represents a private sector response to the inadequacy and underfunding of public sector policy, a response that is not only expensive and inefficient financially, but wasteful and degrading in human terms, as families spend months and even years living in one poorly-appointed room, with longlasting effects on young children's health and education.

The physical condition of the private housing stock has deteriorated during the Thatcher years. Policy on improvement and repair has not kept pace with the rate of decline, while clearance and redevelopment have virtually come to an end (Gibson, 1986). Moreover, the poor physical condition of much of the public sector stock is now becoming apparent. Surveys by the Department of the Environment and the Audit Commission suggest the 85% of the council stock is in need of repair and maintenance, while the total bill required to bring the whole stock up to an acceptable physical standard amounts to almost £20 billion (Department of the Environment, 1985).

It is not only in the rented sector that housing problems exist. In the owner-occupied sector in 1981, 493,000 houses were unfit, and 539,000 were in substantial disrepair (Department of the Environment, 1981). The increase in home ownership coupled with economic recession and the rise in unemployment has meant a rapid growth in the numbers of households falling behind with the mortgage. The numbers of building society repossessions increased from 2500 in 1979 to 21,000 in 1986, while the numbers of mortgages between 6 and 12 months in arrears rose sixfold between 1979 and 1987, from 8400 to 50,400 (Central Statistical Office, 1988).

Widening differentials in house prices, particularly between the North and South (or perhaps 'the rest' and the South-East) have hindered labour mobility, as unemployed workers in the North find it impossible to buy properties in areas where work is more plentiful.

The distribution of housing subsidies has become more inegalitarian. Not only do the majority of councils no longer receive general subsidies, but many now run surpluses on their Housing Revenue Accounts, effectively subsidizing the rates from the 'profits' earned on their council housing. In such areas, ratepayers as a whole thus benefit at the expense of what is likely to be the poorest section of the community (Malpass, 1986).

The unfairness of current housing policies is apparent within, as well as between, tenures. Within the owner-occupied sector, subsidies are distributed so that the biggest benefits go to those who need the least help, i.e. those with the largest mortgages and on the highest incomes, who can claim tax relief at higher rates. Hence, it is existing owners who benefit rather than first-time buyers, higher-income owners rather than lower-income owners, and the South (where both incomes and house prices are higher) rather than the North.

The capitalization of the tax subsidy, and the fact that it is not a subsidy that is linked in any way to *production*, means that much of the assistance given to owner-occupation simply fuels house price inflation as exchange values are bid up. Of course, exchange professionals – estate agents, surveyors and solicitors – benefit through higher commissions, which are usually calculated as a percentage of the house price.

The main effect of Thatcherism in the housing sphere has been to create a new polarization within society. The majority of the population are well-housed, satisfied with their present accommodation and often expect their housing to provide a source of wealth. But there is a substantial minority, perhaps 20 or 30%, which could be termed a new 'underclass', of the homeless and badly-housed, who have little hope of a substantial improvement in the immediate future. Racism, whether overt or hidden, is also a factor, so that a disproportionate number of the homeless and badly-housed are black.

The importance of this division between a moderately well off majority and a deprived underclass and the importance of the housing market in reinforcing it has been remarked on by the sociologist R.E. Pahl (1984:320, 334)

[The] 'middle mass' comprises between 55 and 65 per cent of all households in Britain, with a deprived underclass of between 20 and 25 per cent in poverty beneath them and a well salaried or capital-owning bourgeoisie of about 12–15 per cent above them.... One new element for the future may be the growth in ownership of domestic property among a wider section of the population. The majority of people born after 1970 are likely to inherit a house, or a portion of one, from their parents or grandparents. This seems to be a situation without precedent. Those not owning their dwellings in the year 2000 are likely to be a small, poor and politically ineffective minority.

Thatcher's policies, in actively promoting home ownership at the expense of public rented housing, places severe pressures on people, not only to become owner-occupiers – because that is the only attractive option – but also, once in the housing market, to support policies which preserve the privileges of home owners. In this way, Thatcher's policies increase the divisions in society, and reinforce the polarization between the 'haves' and the 'have nots'. In addition, widespread ownership of domestic property serves to legitimize the notion of private property in general, and thereby weakens support for egalitarian policies which involve an attack on entrenched property interests.

An alternative strategy

What then would an alternative strategy for housing look like in a post-Thatcher Britain? One of the main difficulties in constructing a strategy that is *achievable*, i.e. able to command majority electoral support, is the very growth in polarization outlined above. While it is no exaggeration to talk of a housing crisis in Britain in the 1980s, the Left must also realize that for most households, this is far from their own daily perception of housing conditions. The proportion of households lacking sole use of a bath or shower fell from 12 to 2% between 1977 and 1985. By 1985, 69% of households had central heating, compared with 34% in 1971 (Central Statistical Office, 1988). In 1978, 86% of households were satisfied with their current housing, with only 4% saying they were 'very dissatisfied' (Office of Population Censuses and Surveys, 1980).

We therefore believe it makes sense to divide the question into two: a short-term strategy of the immediate steps that a future left or centre-left government should take to ameliorate the situation, and a long-term strategy based on a radical alternative analysis of the underlying problems. Above all, an alternative view should not be based on attempting blindly to reverse every development since 1979, or simply advocating a return to the 1960s. Profound changes in the housing system and the social structure cannot be ignored and a way must be found to couple an alternative vision with mass electoral support. In order to obtain this support, it will not be enough to appeal solely to the altruistic or egalitarian views of the electorate. A left programme would also need to appeal in some degree to the self-interested motives of the majority in making clear the importance of good housing for all in preserving social peace and maintaining a tolerant and civilized society.

A short-term strategy

By the time a left or centre-left government is elected – possibly in the early 1990s, but more likely the mid-1990s or later – the housing system will be very different from the last time a Labour government came to power in 1974.

The strategy cannot be to solve the housing problem through a massive building programme, not least because the public sector itself will be much reduced. Nevertheless, a left strategy must still be one that is led by the public sector. Central government will need to provide both the commitment and the resources for local authorities to be 'enablers' in the true sense and also to be effective regulators of the system. A left government should not seek to reinstate local authorities as large monolithic providers of housing, with all the complex bureaucracy that entails. Instead, local councils will determine and regulate the context in which a range of organizations build houses, including private house builders, housing cooperatives, housing associations and local authorities themselves.

In the short term particularly, there must be a clear priority of directing help to the more disadvantaged: the homeless and those in the very worst housing conditions. The emphasis should clearly be on raising total output and investment, irrespective of tenure. The shift from a politics of tenure towards one of investment, output and efficiency will be a radical departure from the policies of previous governments, whether Tory or Labour. Yet in many ways, it would simply bring Britain into line with the experience of many other European countries.

Local authorities should be given more freedom to build, not only through relaxing public expenditure controls, but also through allowing capital receipts to be recycled. This will require some redistribution of capital receipts between authorities. Sales of council houses should continue, but with certain amendments. Discounts on the purchase of the current property should be reduced, and the alternative offered of a portable discount on the purchase of a *newly constructed* unit in the private sector, thereby stimulating both private sector investment and re-lets from the existing stock. Also, unless there is demonstrably excess supply in an area, local authorities should be required to replace sales by new units, on a one-for-one basis.

Councils would be expected to devolve decision making and budgetary control to their tenants as far as possible. They should also encourage the activities of democratically based, locally accountable housing associations and support cooperatives. Statutory backing and financial support should be given by central government to tenants' movements.

Local authorities would be encouraged to develop and market their own services in competition with the private sector. For example, repairs departments could offer a contractual maintenance service to owner-occupiers, perhaps starting with owners who have bought properties on council estates under the 'right to buy'. Such activities would build up support for the concept of local, efficient public services.

It would have to be made clear that helping the worst off inevitably involves some redistribution from the better off. However, focussing on investment and the creation of jobs, also benefits the country as a whole, through lowered unemployment and increased GNP. Good housing has positive externalities which benefit the whole community.

The most difficult question is that of housing subsidies, and in particular mortgage interest relief. In the short term, it would not be possible to implement a radical reform of the whole housing finance system immediately. However, it should be made clear that the overall aim of policy is to shift subsidies towards a more tenure-neutral and progressive position. In the council sector, transfers from housing revenue accounts to general rate funds should be banned, and steps taken to ensure that only services of direct benefit to council tenants fall on the Housing Revenue Account. In order to stimulate building by local authorities some general subsidy will be necessary, particularly in high-cost areas such as London.

In the owner-occupied sector, tax relief should be restricted to the basic rate of tax. A capital gains 'surcharge' tax could be introduced on excessive gains through short-term speculation (although there would be obvious difficulties with the definition and collection of such a tax). The incoming government should make it clear that under no circumstances should the ceiling on MIR be raised.

The Treasury accounting conventions should be altered to permit a more realistic assessment of public sector housing activities, distinguishing clearly between investment and consumption expenditure. A housing account should be presented to Parliament annually, which would comprise all housing-related expenditure, including tax expenditures such as mortgage interest relief and capital gains tax exemption, as well as items such as housing benefit which are currently dealt with under other budgetary headings. The global sum could then be monitored in relation to yearly targets and the sizes of the subsidies going to owner-occupied housing would be more clearly visible.

A longer-term strategy

We have argued earlier that it is not enough for the left simply to declare its opposition to Thatcherite policies. There must be a coherent policy *alternative* which tackles the underlying problems and proposes radical solutions. This alternative policy must address both the current housing crisis and the aspirations of the well-housed majority as well as providing a secure basis for future housing improvements.

The underlying problems relate to three areas in particular: land, the house-building industry, and the distribution of wealth and income. The land problem in the UK is complex and can only be touched on here. Land speculation pushes up land values, making it difficult for house building, particularly public sector house building, to compete with other, more profitable uses. It leads to the situation typical in inner cities, whereby large tracts of land are vacant and derelict despite an acute shortage of housing land. Solutions to these problems are necessary to achieve the goal of good housing for all, including the poor. Methods of solving the problem range from extensive public sector land banking, so that as a monopoly owner of land the public sector prevents land values from rising and deters speculation, to site value rating, which makes it costly to hold land unproductively, thereby creating artificial land scarcity and pushing up land values. Both measures, and others, are used with success in other countries including Sweden, the Netherlands, Australia and parts of the USA (Balchin and Bull, 1987).

The second area which must be addressed is the house-building industry. The UK house-building industry is inefficient, compared not only with other sectors of the UK economy, but also with the house-building industries of other advanced economies. While it is always difficult to draw conclusions from international comparisons, in Sweden more houses are built per 1000 population at less cost and of higher quality. This greater efficiency is partly related to the land supply position in Sweden. Swedish local authorities hold land banks and release land to house builders at reasonable cost. In addition, the local authority provides much of the finance during the building period (Duncan, 1985). The main opportunity for profits for house builders, therefore, comes from greater efficiency and productivity. By contrast, in Britain, opportunities exist for considerable profits to be made from land speculation rather than actual construction (Balchin and Bull, 1987).

The third area is the distribution of income and wealth. A redistribution goal is essential to any left programme. Whatever revisions and rethinkings are necessary in the wake of the social and political changes of recent decades, redistribution must lie at the centre of the programme – without it a party or government cannot lay claim to being of the left. There is a two-way relationship between distribution and the housing question. Inequalities of income and wealth lead to unequal access to housing resources, and over-consumption by some while millions are homeless or badly housed. But this is compounded by influences in other directions. Housing is now a major source of wealth in the UK. In the future it is likely that the inheritance of differing amounts of housing equity will be a major factor in perpetuating and reinforcing inequalities of wealth, and thereby access to, for example, private education, private health, or ownership of stocks and shares. A future left government will not be able to avoid tackling the difficult question of the redistribution of housing wealth.

Marxist writers on the left argue that the only long-term solution is nationalization – of land, the housing finance industry and the house-building industry. But a left strategy must acknowledge existing social reality, and the move away from large-scale State enterprises is characteristic not only of Thatcherism, but is a world wide trend, common to such diverse societies as those of France, West Germany, the USSR and China. Therefore, we reject nationalization as not being a viable political strategy in the UK even in the longer term.

Instead, the left must concentrate attention on the issues of promoting greater equality and limiting private sector power. As a set of long-term housing goals we suggest:

1 Greater use of government *regulation* (not ownership) in the areas of land, housing finance and exchange, and the house-building industry.
2 The housing finance system should be tenure neutral. In the long term this means retaining mortgage interest relief but taxing owner-occupiers' imputed rental income (as in the old Schedule A tax) and their real capital gains.
3 Measures such as large-scale public sector land banking should be introduced, keeping down the cost of land and deterring land speculation. Windfall gains from land sales should be taxed in the same way as all other capital gains.
4 The planning system should be reformed to give a greater positive role to planning. Housing policy must be integrated with planning, industrial, regional and urban policies. For example, an overall decision must be taken as to whether the drift of employment and resources to the South-East will be accommodated or reversed in some way. If it is accommodated, then planning controls will have to be released to enable additional housing development to take place. If, on the other hand, the Green Belt is to be preserved, then a strong regional policy will be needed to create jobs in other parts of Britain, and housing investment directed there.
5 Greater public expenditure on housing, both new construction and renewal. The role of housing investment in creating jobs, stimulating local economies and regenerating the inner city should be clearly acknowledged. Estimates of costs and benefits of additional expenditures should reflect these wider social and economic gains.
6 An adequate system of income support for the poorest households, to enable all to have a decent standard of housing, and to avoid the anomalies and poverty trap of the existing housing benefit system. This should be funded partly through revenue obtained from taxing imputed rental income and capital gains as in (2) and (3) above.
7 Adequate financing for housing cooperatives and the tenants' movement.
8 Greater regulation of the building societies will be necessary in the wake of the deregulation of the housing finance market and the likely conversion of some large societies into quasi-banks. Government should have a more directive role, ensuring that a given proportion of the very large funds generated by societies goes towards financing cooperative, voluntary sector and local authority housing projects. The rights of mortgagors and investors in relation to building society managements will need to be strengthened.

This chapter has examined the housing problem under Thatcherism. It has tried to show why despite the flaws and inconsistencies in the ideology of the New Right, Thatcherite housing policies have continued to win political support. That support has its roots in the fact that for perhaps 70% of the population, housing conditions have steadily improved. At the same time the housing system has become more polarized, with a large minority homeless or trapped in bad housing.

An alternative housing strategy must address this polarization, and at the same time face the political realities of the legacy left by Thatcherism. This is no easy task. In the short term, priority must be given to 'crisis management', as the weakened position of local authorities precludes massive public sector house building, however great the need. In the longer term, more fundamental problems have to be tackled. The housing crisis was not caused by Thatcher, and many aspects of the present situation, including the growth in home ownership, would have happened anyway. The underlying causes lie in the nature of the land market, the house-building industry and finance for house building, and the distribution of income and wealth. A New Left government has to address all of these if the housing problem is to be solved.

References

Balchin, P. and Bull, G. (1987). *Regional and Urban Economics*. London: Harper and Row.

Central Statistical Office (1988). *Social Trends*, Vol. 18. London: HMSO.

Clapham, D. and English, J. (eds) (1987). *Public Housing: Current Trends and Future Developments*. London: Croom Helm.

Department of the Environment (1981). *English National House Condition Survey Part 1*. London: HMSO.

Department of the Environment (1985). An Inquiry into the Condition of the Local Authority Housing Stock in England, 1985. Department of Environment. Mimeo.

Duncan, S.S. (1985). Land policy in Sweden: separating ownership from development. In *Land Policy: Problems and Alternatives* (S. Barrett and P. Healey, eds). Aldershot: Gower.

Ermisch, J. (1984). *Housing Finance: Who Gains?* London: PSI.

Forrest, R. and Murie, A. (1988). *Selling the Welfare State: The Privatisation of Public Housing*. London: Routledge and Kegan Paul.

Gibson, M. (1986). Housing renewal: Privatisation and beyond. In *The Housing Crisis* (P. Malpass, ed.). Beckenham: Croom Helm.

Heald, D. (1983). *Public Expenditure*. Oxford: Martin Robertson.

Hepworth, N.P. (1984). *The Future of Local Government*. London: Allen and Unwin.

Heseltine, M. (1980). *Hansard*, 15 January, p. 1445.

Holmans, A.E. (1987). *Housing Policy in Britain*. London: Croom Helm.

Kleinman, M.P. and Whitehead, C.M.E. (1988). British housing since 1979: Has the system changed? *Housing Studies*, **3**, 3–19.

Le Grand, J. and Robinson, R. (1984). *The Economics of Social Problems*. London: Macmillan.

Le Grand, J. and Winter, D. (1987). The Middle Classes and the Welfare State. Welfare State Programme, Discussion Paper No. 14. London: London School of Economics.

Malpass, P. (1983). Residualisation and the re-strucuring of housing tenure. *Housing Review*, March/April, pp. 44–5.

Malpass, P. (1986). Councils that cheat their tenants. *Roof*, May/June, pp. 12–20.

Malpass, P. (1988). Pricing and subsidy systems in British social rented housing: Assessing the policy options. *Housing Studies*, 3(1), 31–9.

Malpass, P. and Murie, A. (1987). *Housing Policy and Practice*, 2nd edition. London: Macmillan.

Musgrave, R.A. (1959). *The Theory of Public Finance*. New York: McGraw-Hill.

National Federation of Housing Associations (1985). *Inquiry into British Housing: Report*. London: NFHA.

Office of Population Censuses and Surveys (1980), *General Household Survey 1978*. London: HMSO.

Pahl, R.E. (1984). *Divisions of Labour*. Oxford: Blackwell.

Shelter (1987). *Housing Monitor*, 2.

Whitehead, C.M.E. and Kleinman, M.P. (1986). *Private Rented Housing in the 1980s and 1990s*. Cambridge: Granta Editions.

10 Law and Order

Mike Brake and Chris Hale

> We will not make law and order an election issue, the British people will (Margaret Thatcher, 1977).

> In their muddled but different ways, the vandals on the picket lines and the muggers in our streets have got the same confused message – 'we want our demands met or else' and 'get out of the way, give us your handbag' (Margaret Thatcher, 1979).

Law and order as a party political issue

In the General Election of 1979 the Tory Party correctly identified 'law and order' as the crystallization of a range of social anxieties, and successfully distinguished itself from the other political parties as alone having solutions to them. It paid particular attention to industrial relations, public order and street crimes, isolating in particular, young black men as the sources, and inner cities as the sites of danger. The mugger on the street became symbolic of the general moral and economic decline of the nation.

At the same time, this apparent 'populism' was inattentive to other areas of 'invisible victimization' and the resulting marginality of victimized groups. Little, if any, discussion, for example, of racist attacks on black people, domestic violence, child abuse (save in terms of protecting the family), sexual assault, police discrimination, attacks on the homosexual community, or for that matter corporate crime, will be found in Tory statements on law and order.

Concentration on the dramas of 'mugging', armed robbery and public disorder has justified shifts towards 'reactive' or 'firebrigade' policing; while at the same time the existence of supposedly dangerous populations has been used to justify disproportionate surveillance as well as punitive sentencing.

Despite more repressive measures to deal with the problem of law and order, recorded crimes have continued to rise since 1979. So far, this has not worked to the Conservatives' disadvantage, but it has led them to redefine the problem. The emphasis has shifted to issues of personal morality and collective responsibilities. In this chapter we will explore some of these issues, concentrating on the consequences of the Conservatives' law and order stance for policing, youth and penal policy.[1]

The changing form of policing in Britain[2]

A rapid transformation of British policing has occurred over the last 20 years (Bowden, 1978; Mark, 1977). In particular, routine policing has become increasingly organized around the imperatives of 'social surveillance' and of quick 'reactive policing' to public incident reports, or requests for assistance. In routine policing, there has been a marked move from traditional versions of neighbourhood-based policing (the bobby on the beat), to the definition of policing as an intensive and technically efficient maintenance of public order.

The 'soft' end of this new policing has involved other community organizations in multi-agency policing. The 'hard' end has seen the rapid creation and expansion of various kinds of specialized quasi-military police units – the Special Patrol Groups (SPG) and the Police Support Units (PSU) – capable of the rapid dispersal of situations threatening public order, which have ranged in the last few years from fights outside public houses and incidents concerning soccer hooliganism, to the prevention of trespass as in the policing of the 'hippy convoy' at Stonehenge, the demonstrations of the Greenham women, the fights with black and white youth during 1980–81 and 1985 and the miners' strike of 1984.

This transformation of image, ideology and form can be traced from several key moments which have occurred in periods of crisis in the economic and political affairs of Britain. The first dates back to the late 1960s with the anti-Vietnam demonstrations in Britain, and the resurgence of the 'troubles' in Northern Ireland. The latter led to close collaboration between the Royal Ulster Constabulary and the British military, both in operations and in intelligence surveillance. It was here that the new technology was first used, and in many ways Ireland has been the testing ground for the introduction of more military types of policing on the mainland.

A second moment involved the national miners' strikes of 1972 and 1984. Organizationally in 1972 the police were hampered by the Police Act of 1964, which only allowed the Chief Constables of the new county forces to request assistance from each other, whereas the National Union of Mineworkers (NUM) were able to organize 'flying pickets' at a national level. The pickets' successful closure of a key industrial installation at Saltley Gap coke depot was seen by the police as a professional defeat which they were determined would not be repeated. A consequence of this was the setting up that year by the Association of Chief Police Officers (ACPO) of the National Reporting Centre (NRC), to centralize information and to organize the PSUs, including the SPGs. The NRC meant that for the purposes of policing national strikes, such as those of the NUM (seen by Mrs Thatcher as 'the enemy within'), the police could mount operations without seeking the approval of the local authority police committees, or indeed Parliament.

Throughout the 1984 miners' strike, legally a civil dispute between the National Coal Board and the NUM, the Government refused to intervene directly, but gave tacit support to police undermining of the workers' effectiveness. Medieval laws were resurrected to allow the police to set up road blocks preventing strike supporters crossing county lines, obscenity laws were used against those verbally abusing strike breakers, and local municipal bye-laws to impose curfews on individual mining communities. Conditions of bail were set in such a way as to prevent pickets from carrying out trade union duties. The effect of this was the criminalization of trade union activity disapproved of by the Government.

The efficiency and speed of police response can be traced to the effectiveness of the NRC computerized information. The police were organized to defend the Orgreave coke plant, working to a recently circulated set of instructions (Public Order Tactical Options) developed by ACPO. This involved incapacitating ringleaders, truncheon charges, chanting and beating riot shields ('tactical use of noise') (*Observer*, 21 July 1985). The NRC, under the supervision of the president of the ACPO, suggested that what had emerged was a national highly organized, politically sophisticated professional organization of police forces. The public image of police chiefs has moved from the presentation of themselves as professional officers without opinions, to making politically sophisticated comments upon morality, accountability and public order, with a confidence suggesting considerable tacit government support.

A third key moment was the events which occurred between the police and the black community. While there had been serious confrontations and lack of confidence in the white police force by the black community since the 1950s, it was the second generation of black Britons which made this public, and to whom the media responded. There had been a series of attacks on Afro-Caribbean and Asian Britons, involving arson, assault and occasionally murder. Black British youth of Afro-Caribbean origins had felt stereotyped as illegal drug dealers and proponents of street crime, and this had led to a moral panic in the 'mugging' issue of the mid-1970s (see Hall *et al.*, 1978). Hall *et al.* argued that a socially anxious and xenophobic society, concerned about the increasing recession, permissiveness (especially in the area of sexuality and drug abuse), and the fading of Britain's international importance, projected its fears about social change and the composition of its population on to the figure of the 'un-British' black 'immigrant', and combined this with its other major 'folk devil' – youth. Consequently, 'mugger' became equated with black youth, and therefore the whole debate has contained a latent racial undertone.

This history of tension between the police and the black community helps us to make sense of the youth 'uprisings' in 1980–81 and 1985. They were a culmination of a series of saturation operations using the SPGs, close surveillance, and raids on social centres and youth clubs. The street riots of 1980–81 occurred in over 40 English cities and towns, where the young unemployed lived, and frequently in districts where saturation policing had been used. While both black and white youth were involved, it was black youth who remained in the memories of the public. The Report of a Commission of Enquiry under Lord Scarman offered criticisms of existing police practices (see Reiner, 1985; Hall, 1982; Lea and Young, 1984). It proposed the disciplining of racist police officers (individualized into 'bad apples'), increased consultation between police forces and local communities, 'lay visits' to local police stations at any time, the independent investigation of serious complaints, and limiting the broad discretion of both individual officers and Chief Constables.

During the 1980s there has been a move towards a more aggressive form of policing. In addition to the incidents mentioned above, there has been the harassment of those carrying out civil disobedience, especially women peace demonstrators at Greenham Common (5000 peace demonstrators were arrested in 1984) using spurious bye-laws, and the 'battle of the bean field', the attack by police on the hippy peace convoy (June 1985). Complaints have been made by gay men and lesbians, who feel since the AIDS publicity that they have been legitimated as targets of assault, particularly since the notorious clause 29 of the Local Government Act.[3] There is a general feeling that the increase of attacks on persons and property of those who are seen as being outside of respectable life, has been tacitly legitimated by the tone of the law and order debate.

The key aspects involving legislation and police organization stem from the Police Act of 1964 and its revisions in the Police and Criminal Evidence Act of 1984 (PACE). The original Royal Commission on

Criminal Procedure 1978, which influenced much of the policy leading to PACE, was set up by Labour, and indeed PACE, which the Conservatives claim sets the 'framework for modern policing with consent', originally came from Labour policies.

The Act, rather than limiting police powers, in fact extended them. It takes note of Lord Scarman's suggestion about obtaining community views on policing, yet the police are not made more accountable to democratic local bodies. Police chiefs have always refused to discuss operations, and most local authorities are not aware when rubber bullets or CS gas have been issued to their local forces. PACE contains no guidelines for reasonable force, and fingerprinting can be enforced, as can the seizure of property and information. In serious offences, the police have the power to detain a person for extended periods, and search their premises even if they are not suspected of a crime. Road blocks can be set up, powers of arrest are increased, and detention without contact can last up to 36 hours. Powers to search, including strip search, are increased, as are stop and search powers. The Act pays heed to the Royal Commission's view that there is a contradiction between 'bringing offenders to justice' and the 'rights and liberties of persons suspected or accused of crime'. The protection of the civil rights and liberties of a person presumed innocent is ignored in the interests of pragmatism. While police accountability is dealt with by the new Police Complaints Authority, the police ultimately still investigate themselves. The crisis of law and order is that now the breakdown in confidence in the police experienced by the black community has spread to the white population. Those marginalized by the criminal justice process are further delegitimated, and the act increases the area of potential abuse, while giving the State further powers.

The media orchestration of folk devils such as football hooligans, unemployed youth and black youth have been joined by an increased variety of those perpetrators of moral panics of differing severity such as 'terrorists', urban criminals, demonstrators and trade unionists. We have come a long way from the time when Sir Robert Mark, the ex-Commissioner of Scotland Yard, wrote of the police:

> The post war years have seen a gradual change in our role from mere role enforcement to participants in the role of social welfare and even more importantly to that of contributors in the moulding of public opinion and legislation (Quoted in Critchley, 1978:4).

Youth and the law and order issue: The emergence of multi-agency policing

One notable change in official attitudes to youth can be seen in the implementation of the Criminal Justice Act of 1982. The Children and Young Persons Act of 1969 was the result of social welfare influence, which argued for the caring rather than the control aspect of juvenile work. It was rehabilitative, non-punitive and treatment-orientated. However, if we examine the juvenile sentencing figures for 1971–81 (see Smith, 1984), we see that in practice measures such as probation, supervision and care orders have declined, while at the same time there has been an increase in punitive measures, especially custody. The Criminal Justice Act 1982 Smith argues, shifts legislative emphasis from treatment to control. What we see here is the 'short sharp shock', illustrated by the introduction of very short detention centre sentences, in as disciplinarian a regime as can be managed. The Act finally disposed of any lingering rehabilitative aspect of the Children and Young Persons' Act 1969. It not only restored to the judiciary the power to commit young persons to prison, a power the earlier Act had severely restricted – at least in principle – but it has also extended the age limit downwards from 17 to 15 years.

A particular strategy which developed was the multi-agency approach to community policing. Indeed, the Government has seen fit to write into the 1986 Education Act a requirement which makes it incumbent on school heads, when discharging their duties to the curriculum, to have regard to any representations made by the chief officer of police and which are connected with his responsibility.

Section 30 of the same Act instructs the school governing body to include in its annual report steps taken to develop links with the police. Menter (1988) has suggested that important developments have taken place in the police/schools debate since 1980, and this involves attempts to develop better relations between the police and local black youth. The stated intention of the programmes is to foster better relations, but this has been challenged by some teachers. They are concerned about police expertise in presenting programmes, and about their hidden motivation – information gathering. The multi-agency approach places teachers in the difficult situation of being seen as extensions of the police surveillance system, and some teachers have argued that the racism left out of the programmes is police racism (Kolenzo, 1984). Policing by consent is partially achieved by policing through ideology, and the school is in the front line of this strategy.

A second agency involved in this approach is the probation service. The courts' loss of confidence in the probation service as an effective measure in crime reduction, led to 50% fewer men being placed on probation between 1969 and 1979. This was due to new alternatives in sentencing, such as suspended and deferred sentences, and community service. One result of this decline was the 'coercive tilt' (Walker and Beaumont, 1981) with suggestions from the service itself to introduce a more controlling form of probation supervision which it was felt would be more attractive to the courts. The Younger Report (Young Adult Offenders, Association of Chief Probation Officers) in 1974 (again under Labour), had suggested probation officers should be given power to detain offenders in custody for 72 hours. Despite the outrage which followed, in 1980 a Probation Control Unit opened for 17- to 24-year-olds in Kent. Its strict regime led to it being closed in 1985. A probation order is an alternative to a custodial sentence, but the 1982 Criminal Justice Act had a provision for offenders to be required to attend a specified place for up to 60 days. The 'short sharp shock' in detention centres, while pandering to the more controlling elements of the law and order supporters in Parliament and on the bench, was found to have little effect on inmates, but a bad effect on uniformed staff morale (Young Offender Psychology Unit, 1984). There was also 'evidence that the trainees actually enjoyed the para-military trappings of the new regimes' (Shaw, 1987). The Home Secretary, Leon Brittan, however, responded by extending the regime to all detention centres.

The 1982 Criminal Justice Act in fact gave magistrates powers to order the removal from home of young people by social services, to sentence young people to Prison Department institutions, and introduced Care Orders with residential conditions. In fact, the bench's response was to increase custodial sentences to the degree that the Appeal Court in reality laid down guidelines for custodial sentencing under the Act (Whitehead and MacMillan, 1985; Cavadino, 1985). Curfews were possible as a condition of probation or social service supervision, but the professional social work unions refused to implement these.

Other surveillance techniques have been introduced for young people. Tracking (Brockington and Shaw, 1986), as an alternative to custodial sentences, was introduced from the USA into this country in the late 1970s. Again it met resistance from professional social workers who disliked the punitive element it might introduce into their work. It has not proved popular with social services and probation services and, in the small numbers of cases where tracking has been introduced, it has usually developed as part of a supervision order. The tracking schemes which have been used in Medway, Leeds and Coventry also provide little evidence as to its superiority over other forms of intervention.

Penal policy and the prison programme

One sign of success in the fight for law and order is that more people are in prison (Merlyn Rees, former Home Secretary, quoted in Gilroy and Sim, 1985).

In 1979, the incoming Conservative Government inherited a crisis in the prisons system. The Report of the Work of the Prison Department, (1979) showed that the average daily prison population for that year was 42,220, with a peak figure of 43,036. Both of these were the highest on record, but by March 1980 the prison population had reached a new high of 44,800 (NACRO Briefing, 1980). The average daily population of unconvicted and unsentenced prisoners rose by nearly 9% in 1979, after a 7% rise in 1978. Approximately one-third of these prisoners were found not guilty, or did not receive a prison sentence after trial (NACRO Briefing, 1980). These figures do not show that behind them 'lie some of the most unsatisfactory conditions for any prisoners'.

William Whitelaw was more guarded in his reaction to these figures than Merlyn Rees, when he gave the Government's response to the May Report to the House of Commons on 30 April 1980. In the weeks preceding the announcement he had been told, in unequivocal terms from several quarters, of the state of overcrowding in Britain's prisons. On 21 March, for example, a delegation from the Prison and Borstal Governors branch of the Society of Civil and Public Servants submitted to him a seven-point programme to deal with the prison crisis in which they stated:

> Governors have a duty to warn the country that the prison system at this very moment is collapsing under the weight of numbers. We need the support of all those concerned about law and order to urge the Government to take action.

The Government had already accepted in full the May Report's proposals on pay. Mr Whitelaw stated that the Government would welcome the 'exercise of judicial discretion' to ensure shorter sentences for non-violent offenders and would continue to give full support to the development of non-custodial alternatives to prison. Further, two new major prison building projects were planned for 1981–2 and 1982–3 to provide 1500 places by the late 1980s. This dichotomy of encouragement for more lenient sentences and non-custodial sentences was to distinguish Tory penal strategy up to the present day.

Ironically, the Government's 'short sharp shock' experiment, the only major innovation suggested in the 1979 manifesto, has also failed to help reduce the incarcerated population. As noted above, the tougher regimes seem to have been a failure. Following the extension of their powers in 1983, under the 1982 Criminal Justice Act, magistrates preferred to use the longer youth custody training sentences, rather than the shorter even if sharper shocks. As Shaw (1987), notes: 'In contrast to the grievous overcrowding in much of the prison system, many detention centres have been little more than half full.' The overall effect of this has been to increase the average numbers of young people in custody.

By 1986-7, the average prison population was 47,200, reaching a total of 49,000 on 31 March. This was an increase of 1200 compared to the average of the previous year and was mainly due to an increase in the number of untried and unsentenced prisoners, and prisoners serving longer sentences (Report on the work of the Prison Service 1986-7). Certified Normal Accommodation (CNA) for prisons was 41,650, a rise of 450 from the previous year. The gap between CNA and actual population was in the region of 7500. Consequently, more prisoners were held two or three in a cell, and more in police cells (190) (NACRO Briefing, 1988). The situation is clearly deteriorating: by 19 February 1988 the number of prisoners in England and Wales stood at 49,979, of which 1260 were held in police and court cells because of the lack of space in prisons. The CNA had increased to 42,546 indicating a slight improvement in overcrowding! Even allowing for the seasonal fluctuations which give rise to peak figures around Easter, there were 1400 more prisoners than at the same time in 1987. What makes these figures even more striking is that on 13 August 1987, remission on sentences of 12 months or less was increased from one-third to half the sentence. This change reduced the prison population by over 3000 - it fell from 51,019 on 7 August to 47,918 on 14 August. Without this change, therefore, the prison population would have increased by 4500 on the previous year.

Meanwhile, in a more desperate attempt to solve the problem of overcrowding, new prisons are being built in the largest expansion programme undertaken this century. Twenty-six new prisons between 1983 and 1995 will be provided, at an estimated total capital cost of £870 million at 1987 prices. This is expected to provide 17,500 new places in all, at an average cost per place of £69,200.[4] In the shorter term, the Home Secretary has again made use of Army camps and Army personnel, Rollestone Army camp being used as a temporary expedient from August to October 1987 and, along with Camberley, reopened in March 1988 to house a total of about 700 prisoners. According to the Home Secretary in a debate on the (continuing) crisis in prisons, 'This will be a strictly temporary measure to bridge us through the summer until more permanent prison accommodation is available.' In addition, he again raised the possibility of involving the private sector in prison building and management, and in privately managed bail hostels. He re-emphasized that the Government's role was to provide prison places, not to interfere with the judicial process, echoing his words of November 1987:

> It is not for the Home Secretary, government or the House to lay down to the courts how many people they send to prison. It is our job to provide places for them (*Hansard*, 5 November, 1987, Column 1055).

Again, however, he stated his aim to provide the courts with more persuasive options outside prison. He committed the Government to encouraging expansion in the number of day centres and providing for many more projects, stressing once more their apparent keenness to support the development of community service orders.

However, despite the fact that Home Office Ministers have argued consistently since 1979 that prisons should be used only for violent or serious offenders and despite the expansion of prison accommodation, the Government is clearly not coping with the numbers being incarcerated. To discover why in practice they have failed to reduce the prison population, we need briefly to examine some of the measures which have been proposed since Mrs Thatcher became Prime Minister. For example, in 1981 William Whitelaw proposed to reduce the prison population by an estimated 7000 through granting parole after one-third of a prison sentence. But the Magistrates Association Sentencing of Offenders Committee strongly opposed this move and threatened to retaliate by committing more offenders to Crown Court for sentencing, a move calculated to secure longer sentences to offset early parole. By mid-1982 the plan was dropped and instead partially suspended sentences created under Section 47 of the Criminal Law Act 1977 were introduced.

The Criminal Justice Act 1982 abolished imprisonment for the offence of loitering for the purpose of prostitution – simple drunkenness was removed from the list of offences punishable by imprisonment by the Criminal Justice Act of 1977. The net result was that more people ended in prison as fine defaulters, especially after the Home Secretary announced in 1984 that maximum fines in magistrates' courts were to be doubled.

The introduction of the partially suspended sentence noted above also failed to achieve a reduction in the prison population. Home Office researchers examined 500 partially suspended sentences imposed in the first quarter of 1982, and concluded that 'possibly up to half these sentences replaced full sentences of imprisonment, or non-custodial sentences' (Dean 1983).

This is yet another example of how attempts to decrease the use of imprisonment by offering non-custodial sentences have the effect instead of increasing the total numbers in the custodial system, while not affecting the numbers in prison at all. Instead of individuals moving down tariff the judiciary have used any alternatives made available to them for people who would previously have received lighter sentences, or been let off completely.

A similar fate will almost certainly await intermittent (or weekend) imprisonment when and if it is introduced. The Magistrates Association have already made it plain that their members intend to use this sentence as an *extra* custodial sanction rather than an alternative to a 6-month (or less) sentence. The net effect, according to the Association of Chief Probation Officers, will be to increase again the number of persons in prison (Dean, 1984). Only by legislating for shorter sentences and diverting resources from the prison building programme towards non-custodial alternatives will any real reduction in the prison population be achieved (for a further discussion, see Box and Hale, 1986).

Conservative law and order: What next?

In one sense, law and order can be seen as the Conservative confidence trick of the 1980s, yet in another, as suggested above, it is an integral part of their success. In their 1979 election manifesto, they argue:

> The number of crimes in England and Wales is nearly half as much again as it was in 1973. The next Conservative government will spend more on fighting crime even while we economise elsewhere (Conservative Party, 1979).

They have certainly not failed to meet that pledge. In 1978–9 expenditure on the police was £1.1 billion, by 1986–7 it was £3.2 billion, an increase of 51%, after allowing for inflation. A major prison building programme has been planned and implemented. However, the implicit promise to reduce crime has palpably failed, if the official figures used by the Tories themselves are to be believed. Between 1980 and 1986 there was a 45% increase in the numbers of notifiable offences reported to the police (Criminal Statistics, 1986). Using rates per 100,000, the average annual change in serious crimes known to the police was 7.5% between 1979 and 1986, compared to 4.2% between 1974 and 1979. Furthermore, the national clear up rate was 41.3% in 1979 but had fallen to 31.6% by 1986, a drop of nearly 25%. Clearly, the tough policies and increased expenditure had not had their desired effect, and this has not escaped notice within the Government.

Mr Hurd, in a speech to the General Synod of the Church of England (February 1988), noted that the level of violent crime 'has risen at a relentless rate of some 5.7 per cent a year .. despite an unrivalled effort to strengthen the police service and toughen the sentences available to the court'. The point is also made by Clarke and Hough (1984:1), who after reviewing the research literature, conclude that 'crime will not be significantly reduced by devoting more manpower to conventional police strategies'. Not surprisingly, this lack of 'value for money' has led to a subtle shift in Government statements on the issue since the 1983 election. In its 1987 manifesto, there is a more cautious approach to crime, and the admission that 'Government alone cannot tackle such deep rooted problems easily or quickly.' The emphasis has moved from simply extolling the virtues of strong police powers and tougher sentencing to curb crime. Now the problem is seen as a crime rate which has been rising steadily over the years, not just in Britain but most other countries too, and so not to be seen as an indication of government failure.

The source of the problems of crime and violence are firmly located:

deep in society: in families where parents do not support or control their children; in schools where discipline is poor; and in the wider world where violence is glamorised and traditional values are under attack (Conservative Party, 1987).

It is not government economic policy with high unemployment and a sizeable population living below the poverty line which is seen as affecting crime, but 'indiscipline, slovenliness and warped social attitudes' (*Politics Today*, 1988:48). The law and order issue is removed from the political economy into the realms of individual morality and pathology. Mrs Thatcher reminded us that what was needed was to:

restore a clear ethic of personal responsibility – we need to establish that the main person to blame for each crime is the criminal (Speech to the Annual Conference of Conservative Officers, March 1988).

If anyone else is to blame, she continued:

it is the professional progressives among broadcasters, social workers and politicians who have created a fog of excuses in which the mugger and the burglar operate.

Gradually, Government speakers, as well as reiterating continued commitment to the police and prison building programmes, are also raising the idea that the police cannot continue without public support. The way forward they suggest, is through crime prevention programmes argued for in a series of papers published by the Home Office Research and Planning Unit. This campaign implicitly suggests that not much can be done about the fact that people will commit crimes, and focusses instead on reducing the opportunity to do so.

The Neighbourhood Watch schemes, which are at the centre of this approach, numbered some 42,000 and covered an estimated 3.5 million households by February 1988 (*Politics Today*, 1988:35). The Government claim that these schemes are making a major contribution to crime reduction and quote impressive figures to back their claims. What is clear is that Neighbourhood Watch is a predominantly middle-class phenomenon. As Hough and Mayhew (1985:49) point out in their review of the British Crime Survey, the person most likely to be involved is 'a man, in a non manual job, on an average or above-average salary, living with his wife and children, as an owner occupier, in a modern house'. Moreover, Bennett (1987) has recently found that such schemes have little impact upon victimization rates, and that reporting and clear up rates changed very little. Crime rates are highest in the type of neighbourhood which is in the most deprived areas, where lack of interest in the scheme prevents its implementation.

Victim support schemes have also grown under the Thatcher Government. Basically, volunteers follow up victims of crimes to discuss their feelings and offer advice. However, they are hampered (Maguire and Corbett, 1986) by overloading of the co-ordinators, as the scheme becomes successful; too much reliance on police decisions as to who should be visited; and lack of long-term help for the most psychologically damaged. The situation is further exacerbated by underfunding which leads to overloading the workers.

These schemes attempt to involve the community in crime prevention and victim support, but depend on a large pool of volunteers, and are often not managed efficiently. While they follow government inclinations to privatization and community involvement in crime prevention their success is limited to neighbourhoods which contain individuals with spare time, energy and skills. In other words, like the Neighbourhood Watch Schemes, they have been successful in middle-class rather than working-class neighbourhoods, and have had little impact in high crime areas.

Alternatives to right-wing law and order policies

There has been an attempt in the 1980s to construct viable socialist policies and strategies around the issue of law and order. This is a complex issue for radicals, since they must steer a course between what Young (1986) calls the 'impossibilism' of 'left wing idealism' and the authoritarian tendencies of the right. Clearly, this is an issue which affects the working class disproportionately, because the street crimes sensationalized by the media are (notwithstanding the protestations of Douglas Hurd), committed by the working class on the working class. Therefore, any solution which offers nothing more than awaiting a socialist Utopia when crime, like alienation, will disappear both ignores the concrete reality as experienced by many and leaves open (indeed has surrendered) the ideological terrain to the right. As Schofield (1985:44) argues:

It is the contradictory nature of working class crime which needs to be understood in so far as the crimes themselves are a form of rebellion, but the impact on the victims is reactionary and turns the practical energy for social transformation into inertia, or even tacit support for state authoritarianism.

A new approach, which may be called 'left realism', a title adopted by Lea and Young (1984), (although many of the authors we refer to might not agree with the title or parts of the programme), has at its core the idea that crime has a material reality, particularly for working-class communities. Socialists must address these issues and put forward programmes which improve the situation in the short term. The left idealist view for Lea and Young is that view which argues the State is a class State, of which the police are functionaries concerned with the repression of radical struggle. Crime is often latent political struggle criminalized by the State and the media. Lea and Young posit the view of 'left realism' which assumes: 'we need a police force because crime is a real problem. There is a lot of it and it harms the working class community' (Lea and Young, 1984:259). Basically, this view argues that while the State is clearly dominated in the present situation by the right, it remains a key site of struggle, and that the policies of Thatcherism can be successfully challenged by alternative political and social programmes which attempt to address economic reality and the political consciousness of present-day Britain.

In doing so, however, it is important to remind ourselves that no matter how responsible and accountable the police may become, and no matter how humane the prison system, they are nevertheless part of the apparatus of a State which is responsible for maintaining control in the interests of capital. Working-class assumption of power is the prerequisite of any real democratization of policing and the judicial process. The basic view of the left realist thinkers is that crime, not criminals, is the problem. They suggest that the emphasis on crime and the drift to the law and order society is a predictable and rational response to the recessionary crisis. Where rewards and social justice cannot be offered, then control through the certain administration of punishment must prevail.

The left-wing response involves resurrecting the rehabilitative model instead of the punitive one. It aims at the demarginalization of crime by several preventative measures which will reduce public hysteria about crime. One aspect is to include the local community in preemptive deterrence, by arguing that it is better to prevent crime rather than punish the offender afterwards. This means programmes which organize responses on a neighbourhood level, rather than merely focussing on individual suspicious actions. Lea and Young argue for organizing within the community, including local police forces. Better police community relations, and more democratic police accountability are part of this strategy, and this means rethinking community policing. It is apparent, however, that at the present time considerable police community trust would have to be recovered, if this is to be viable.

Situational crime prevention programmes (Hudson, 1987) have also been suggested, although these differ from the Conservative suggestions because they are located in plans for wider structural changes, so that local programmes are contextualized in wider strategies to combat unemployment, poverty and deprivation. It is argued that these developments will counteract the marginalization of the dispossessed, so that they become less involved in criminal acts of theft, violence and vandalism. A further element important in left-wing alternatives is that of community regeneration. This requires improving whole neighbourhoods and includes safer transport services, better lighting and more sympathetic architecture so that areas become less vulnerable to street crime.

The final strategy is to reduce the prison population, which marginalizes and excludes the prisoner rather than integrating him or her into the community. This could happen by the use of more part-time sentences, community service orders or by victim restitutive programmes. The latter recognizes a victim's right to proper recompense, and attempts to bring about mediations between victim and offender. The minimal use of prison would reduce its population and provide funding for alternatives.

If we want to look at alternative social crime prevention programmes, we need to consider some of Europe's experiments. France has invested something like Fr45 million a year on crime prevention projects such as the inner-city *été-jeunes* programmes. Holland has set aside £15 million for local experimental projects, and both Sweden and West Germany have prioritized crime prevention programmes among juveniles (Home Office Research Bulletin, **24**, 1988).

Crime, like poverty and unemployment, has a material base. The dispossessed in our society are not only more likely to be involved in crime, but they are also more likely to be victims of crime. The controversial, hidden agenda in discussions about criminal statistics is race. There is a debate about the presence of ethnicity in criminal statistics, and given that these are socially constructed, how much they reflect merely the police disapproval and tight surveillance of black youth. However, as Stevens and Willis (1979) suggest, being a working-class adolescent is a greater predictor of crime than ethnicity, and all that a high black presence in the statistics indicates, is that black people are more likely to be imprisoned than white people. Racist attacks on black people are notably absent from the crime statistics, and the fear and distress of racism as a daily event in the lives of black people is something of which many white people are ignorant.

The law and order debate needs to move beyond the agenda set by the right, not least because the Conservative Government has conspiciously failed to reduce crime. While legitimating punitive attitudes it ignores corporate crime, white collar crime, domestic violence, racist attacks, discriminatory police treatment and its consequent violence, prosecutions arising from welfare provision, pornography and the treatment of gay men and lesbians. It is time the right's law and order programmes were revealed for what they really are – a serious threat to civil liberties while being totally ineffective in the fight against crime. However, they are currently proposing further inroads into civil liberties by suggesting the introduction of identity cards and the building of private detention centres for remand prisoners.

The swing to the right is an authentic response to the problems of crime and lawlessness but is not the only possible one. Labour now needs to attack the populist moralism which has replaced rehabilitative and progressive ideas. Such organizations as NACRO, the NCCL and the Labour Campaign for Criminal Justice possess a repertoire of radical ideas. Labour needs to move away from a hawkish stand which imitates Tory policy, and to offer workable alternatives such as shorter sentencing, better police accountability, more use of the parole system and the exploration of alternatives to imprisonment. Obviously, the law and order issue has to be contextualized as part of a broad-based agenda for reform which is based on thorough-going socialist principles. The municipal Labour Parties have set up and managed successful police monitoring schemes and have started debates between local communities and their police forces. These are local responses, but they are the roots of national policies which could offer a radical response to current anxieties. There is a considerable amount of literature about law and order from a socialist perspective, which the left could use to address seriously the current issues. It is a debate which could be won at the next election, and which could provide the basis of a reasoned collective response, not only in the arena of law and order, but also in other areas of State provision such as health, education and social services. These are also areas suffering from the injustices of Thatcherism, which is resulting in an increasing proportion of the population becoming economically impoverished and politically and socially marginalized.

Notes

1 We can only hope to raise some of the issues of this debate in a chapter of this length, but for a more thorough investigation, see Brake and Hale (in press).
2 Much of this section is based on a considerably revised paper originally given by Michael Brake and Ian Taylor at the American Criminological Association at Cincinnati in 1984.

3 Clause 29 of the Local Government Act prevents the presentation of homosexuals in educational institutions maintained by the local authority as positive role models, or as part of a 'pretended family unit'.
4 Written Parliamentary Answer from the Earl of Caithness, the then Minister of State at the Home Office, 9 December 1987 (NACRO Briefing, 1988).

References

Bennett, T. (1987). *Evaluation of Two Neighbourhood Watch Schemes in London*. Cambridge: Institute of Criminology.

Bowden, T. (1978). *Beyond the Limits of the Law*. Harmondsworth: Penguin.

Box, S. and Hale, C. (1986). Unemployment, crime and imprisonment, and the enduring problem of prison overcrowding. In *Confronting Crime* (R. Matthews and J. Young, eds). London: Sage.

Brake, M. and Hale, C. (in press). *Conservative Criminology*. London: Routledge and Kegan Paul.

Brockington, N. and Shaw, M. (1986). Tracking the trackers. *Home Office Research Bulletin*, **27**, 37–40.

Cavadino, P. (1985). Clearer law. *Community Care*, 28 November.

Clarke, J. and Hough, M. (1984). Crime and police effectiveness. *Home Office Research Unit*, **79**.

Conservative Party (1979). *Conservative Party Manifesto*. London: Conservative Central Office.

Conservative Party (1987). *Conservative Party Manifesto*. London: Conservative Central Office.

Criminal Statistics (1986). Cmnd No. 233, London: HMSO.

Critchley, T.A. (1978). *A History of the Police in England and Wales*. London: Constable.

Dean, M. (1983). Figures show misuses of partly suspended sentences. *The Guardian*, 11 November.

Dean, M. (1984). Brittan puts forward plan for weekend imprisonment. *The Guardian*, 30 June.

Gilroy, P. and Sim, J. (1985). Law, order and the state of the left. *Capital and Class*, **25**, 15–51.

Hall, S. (1982). The Scarman Report. *Critical Social Policy*, **2**(2), 66–72.

Hall, S., Chrichter, C., Jefferson, T., Clarke, J. and Roberts, S. (1978). *Policing the Crisis*. London: Macmillan.

Hough, M. and Mayhew, P. (1985). *The British Crime Survey*. London: HMSO.

Hudson, B. (1987). *Justice through Punishment*. London: Macmillan.

Kolenzo, E. (1984). Police in schools. *Challenging Racism*.

Lea, J. and Young, J. (1984). *What is to be Done about Law and Order*. Harmondsworth: Penguin.

Maguire, M. and Corbett, C. (1986). Victim support schemes. *Home Office Research Unit*, **12**.

Mark, R. (1977). *In the Office of Constable*. London: Collins.

Matthews, R. and Young, J. (eds) (1986). *Confronting Crime*. London: Sage.

Menter, I. (1988). The long arm of education: A review of recent documents on police/school liaison. *Critical Social Policy*, **21**, 68–77.

NACRO Briefing (1980). National Association for the Care and Rehabilitation of Offenders, London, September.

NACRO Briefing (1988). National Association for Care and Rehabilitation of Offenders, London, March.

Politics Today (1988). No. 2. London: Conservative Party Research Department.

Reiner, R. (1985). *The Politics of the Police*. Brighton: Wheatsheaf.

Schofield, T. (1985). *Imprisonment on the Political Platform*. MA dissertation, Sheffield City Polytechnic.

Shaw, S. (1987). Whatever happened to the short sharp shock? *The Guardian*, 2 September.

Smith, D. (1984). Law and order, arguments for what? *Critical Social Policy*, **11**.

Stevens, P. and Willis, C. (1979). Race, crime and arrests. *Home Office Research Unit*, **58**.

Walker, H. and Beaumont, B. (1981). *Probation Work, Critical Theory and Socialist Practice*. Oxford: Blackwell.

Whitehead, P. and MacMillan, J. (1985). Checks or blank cheque? *Probation Journal*, September.

Young, J. (1986). The failure of criminology: The need for a radical realism. In *Confronting Crime* (R. Matthews and J. Young, eds). London: Sage.

Young Offender Psychology Unit (1984). *Tougher Regimes in Detention Centres*. London: HMSO.

Subject Index

Name Index